Aging in Literature

A Reader's Guide

by
Robert E. Yahnke
and
Richard M. Eastman

AMERICAN LIBRARY ASSOCIATION

Chicago and London

1990

Cover and text designed by Ray Machura

Composed by Point West, Inc. on a Compugraphic Quadex
5000 and output on a Compugraphic 9600 laser
typesetter in Sabon

Printed on 50-pound Lynx Opaque, a pH-neutral stock,
and bound in 10-point Carolina cover stock by
Imperial Printing Company

The paper used in this publication meets the minimum requirements of American
National Standard for Information Sciences—Permanence of Paper for Printed Library
Materials, ANSI Z39.48-1984. ∞

Library of Congress Cataloging-in-Publication data

Yahnke, Robert E.
    Aging in literature : a reader's guide / Robert E. Yahnke, Richard M. Eastman.
      p. cm.
    Includes index.
    ISBN 0-8389-0551-X (alk. paper)
      1. Old age in literature—Bibliography.   2. Aging in literature—Bibliography.
    3. Aged in literature—Bibliography.   I. Eastman, Richard M.   II. Title.
    Z6514.C50423   1990
    [PN56.04]   90-40192
    016.809′ 93354—dc20   CIP

Printed in the United States of America.

94 93 92 91 90   5 4 3 2 1

Contents

Preface

We have written AGING IN LITERATURE: A READER'S GUIDE because literature on the subject of aging has come of age. More and more writers are portraying the experience of aging in their fiction, drama, poetry, and autobiography. They are creating main characters who are old. They are setting forth plots that show older people dealing firsthand with the issues of later life. They are articulating themes that express some "truths" about old age.

In short, we believe that the subject of old age in literature has long been undervalued, and that a substantial body of literature has been underused by librarians, teachers, gerontologists, and health-care professionals, not to mention the serious general reader.

Previous Guides

Constance E. Kellam provided the first reference text to literature and aging in her 1968 *A Literary Bibliography on Aging.*

When Walter G. Moss wrote *Humanistic Perspectives on Aging: An Annotated Bibliography* in 1976, he noted, "The study of literature as it depicts older people or is written by them can also make a major contribution to gerontology." He called for the development of a "humanistic gerontology" that would contribute to "making a society receptive to a positive attitude toward aging, and making a good society for older people."

Both of these texts broke ground by listing numerous novels, stories, poems, and other literary works that could illuminate aging. Annotations were limited to one or two sentences.

Mary Sohngen's 1977 article in *The Gerontologist,* "The Experience of Old Age as Depicted in Contemporary Novels," added her notations of 87 titles published between 1950 and 1975. She followed this in 1978 with "Images of Old Age in Poetry" (with Robert J. Smith), tabulating various qualities in 127 poems.

In 1981 the National Retired Teachers Association and the American Association of Retired Persons compiled *Learning about Aging,* a bibliography that devoted one of six chapters to "Aging and the Literary Arts." The compilers included some forty entries, mostly novels, and for each, added a brief summary and evaluation (usually one sentence long).

Then in 1983 Margaret E. Monroe and Rhea Joyce Rubin compiled *The Challenge of Aging: A Bibliography,* the most comprehensive text since Moss's 1976 work. It is a useful tool for locating a variety of guides to aging, including more than a hundred titles in its Creative Literature sections. Annotations are slightly longer than in the earlier bibliographies.

A brief 1985 booklet, *Sixty Plus: Seniors in Contemporary Fiction,* has been compiled by Donalda Putnam and published in Ottawa, Ontario, by the Canadian Library Association. It lists 87 titles with a paragraph of commentary to each, some quite brief.

Aging with Style and Savvy (American Library Association, 1990) is a general guide to aging which devotes some sixty pages to literary and film resources with summaries ranging from a few lines to half a page.

About This Guide

Our own first aim has been to expand the evaluative commentary for each item on a scale well beyond that of the former guides. Each annotation provides not only a summary of the literary work but also an appraisal of its relevance to an understanding of aging. To realize this aim for some 150 literary works, we sacrificed a number of entries for quality of treatment. We regretfully but necessarily omitted many titles of potential value, and will look for a later chance to bring more of them to general attention.

In addition, we have provided an index to guide the user to those pieces that focus on given gerontological topics (e.g., Alzheimer's, bereavement, life review).

Because the life attitudes of aging persons are so critical to understanding them and caring for them, we have also provided an appendix, Major Life Responses, that guides the user to pieces portraying such basic attitudes as creativity, reconciliation, rage, boredom.

In short, we hope that our text will stimulate the interest of widely varied readers who want to learn directly about the experience of aging. To study this literature will not confer gerontological expertise. We have gerontology courses and research centers for that. What literature can do is to create, in its readers, the overall experiences of aging—the concrete living situations, the fears and courage and faiths that mark the later years. Gerontology textbooks convey information and judgment; it is not their function to convey the throbbing pulse of actual lives. Yet imaginative literature, though short on science, perhaps can stimulate the student of gerontology to press into areas that have hitherto seemed gray and abstract.

Five Ways to Use This Guide

Within each section, names of authors are listed alphabetically by last name. But within the entry for an author, titles (if more than one) are listed in order of their evident value for an understanding of aging. Thus W. H. Auden's poem "Old People's Home" (entry 401) is listed before "Doggerel by a Senior Citizen" (entry 402).

1. To sample the variety, browse through the main text where some 150 literary texts are described so as to suggest themes and topics of special relevance to an understanding of aging. Entries are numbered and appear in order: the 100 series for novels, the 200s for short stories, the 300s for plays, the 400s for poems, and 500s for nonfiction.

2. To search for entries written by a specific author, scan the List of Entries within Chapters or consult the Index of Authors. Thus the listing under "Sarton, May," will yield the following entries: 124, the novel *As We Are Now;* 430 and 431, the poems "Gestalt at Sixty" and "On a Winter Night"; and 514, the journal *At Seventy.*

3. To find what literary works might show how aging persons respond to their own aging, consult the appendix Major Life Responses. Such broad headings as Love, Hate, Faith, Despair, etc. will be found subdivided with examples and cross-listings to the main text. Thus you might find under "Love" that the theme "friendship" among aged persons is exemplified in item 241, Alice Munro's "Mrs. Cross and Mrs. Kidd," and cross-listed to seven other literary works.

4. To find what literary works treat such gerontological topics as retirement homes, ethnic culture, Alzheimer's disease, etc., consult the Index. Thus the entry "Alzheimer's" would refer you to item 508, Rosalie Honel's nonfiction work, *Journey with Grandpa: Our Family's Struggle with Alzheimer's Disease,* as well as titles 202, 242, 257, and 261.

5. To find what literary anthologies are now available for extending the interests of this guide, see the appendix Anthologies.

Bibliographic Note

For stories and poems, the dates of original publication, when available, are noted in parentheses, to encourage the reader's awareness of history in the portraiture of aging.

Most of these shorter entries appear in collections which, unless otherwise noted, are by the same author. For anthologies the editor of the anthology is noted.

We have tried to point the user to generally reliable editions and collections; but the general user need not insist upon locating the same edition or collection. Many of these titles are so well known as to appear in other usable editions or collections as well.

Novels

101   *Author:* Achebe, Chinua
     Title: **Things Fall Apart** (1958). New York: Astor-Honor, 1959
     Genre: novel
     Commentary: This African novel pays much attention to the customs, myths, and values of the clan. What makes *Things Fall Apart* relevant to the contemporary study of aging is the central tragedy of a strong man secure in traditional values that are falling apart in a cultural revolution. The decline of the man is intensified by the decline of the society.

     Here is an aging leader who tries to stem the break-up of his tribal culture (Ibo, Nigerian) as the white man takes over the clan, first through missionaries and then through armed government. The time is presumably late nineteenth and early twentieth century.

     The central character is Okonkwo, a strong, silent, self-made man who partly because of the weakness of his father aspires to show the full strength of the tribal values. He rises fast to become one of the chief men of his village, but after accidentally killing someone through the discharge of his gun at a celebration, he must go into seven years of exile. This setback prevents him from using his full energies against the incoming white man, especially because he is a guest of his mother's clan when the first missionary appears.

     The white missionaries thrive, first absorbing the marginal natives, then an occasional man of importance. Resistance is crushed by the armed might of the nearby white government. Okonkwo is enraged at the weakening of his own people and single-handedly commits a climactic and ruinous act of violence.

102   *Author:* Amis, Kingsley
     Title: **The Old Devils** (1986). New York: Summit, 1987
     Genre: novel
     Commentary: The title refers to a group of four Welsh married couples in their sixties who have known each other most of their lives and who now face the prospect of new adventures when two of their former friends, Alun and Rhiannon Weaver, move back to Wales after thirty-five years' residence in London. Alun is a writer

and television personality, the inheritor of the great Welsh literary tradition embodied by the works of the famous poet Brydan (probably based on Dylan Thomas).

The relationships of all of the married couples are characterized by a lack of trust, affection, and intimacy. The women spend their days eating, drinking, and gossiping at each others' houses. The men withdraw daily to the neighborhood pubs to seek solace in eating, drinking, and gossiping.

Most of the characters have become caricatures of themselves. Amis portrays, often humorously, these characters' encounters with the physical shortcomings of old age. But they are fearful of facing the psychological reality of their old age. Instead, they remain embroiled in petty jealousies, longstanding disputes, and unresolved relationships that have persisted into old age.

Alun, for example, is more concerned with maintaining his legend as a famous Welsh literary personality than continuing to refine his skills as a writer. His mean spirit and selfishness undermine his popularity. As a man who lives by his reputation, he is not afraid to seduce the wives of some of his friends. Late in the novel he spitefully mistreats one of his old friends who tries to warn him that his writing style is artificial and pretentious.

The two characters who show most promise of personal development are Alun's wife, Rhiannon, and Peter, one of their old friends. Rhiannon has learned to cope with her husband's self-centered, insecure behavior. Although she is aware of his limitations, she cares deeply for him and tries to encourage him to keep working as a writer. Peter's life is made miserable by his boorish wife, who bullies him relentlessly. He is a former lover of Rhiannon's, and eventually he works up the courage to leave his wife.

At the end of the novel, after Alun's sudden death by heart attack, Rhiannon's daughter and Peter's son marry. Amis suggests that in their marriage they will not repeat the mistakes that have deadened the marriages of the "old devils." The new start afforded this young couple is paralleled by Rhiannon and Peter's renewed commitment to each other. Their new life together is the realization of a second chance for these former lovers.

103 *Author:* Anderson, Jessica.
Title: **Tirra Lirra by the River** (1978). New York: Penguin, 1984
Genre: novel
Commentary: Nora Porteus, a woman in her seventies, returns to take occupancy of her mother's home 600 miles from Sydney, Aus-

tralia. Although Nora was born and raised in Australia, she has lived in London for most of her life. Upon arriving at her mother's home, she begins to review her life. Nora's story is subtly rendered through the combination of life review and the narrative in the present. We gain insights into the complexity of an old person's interior world. We see how memory brings to the surface unexpected, compelling revelations about past feelings, relationships, and griefs. Through her life review, Nora relives several deeply felt experiences that illuminate the strengths of her character and provide some perspective on a life that has been lived primarily for others—not for herself.

Nora's inward, psychological journey is complemented by her outward, physical progress. Upon arrival she is bedridden; with the aid of neighbors and a young doctor, who is the son of a childhood friend, Nora begins to establish some familiarity with and eventually control over her environment. Nora finds answers in these physical and psychological journeys: some tentative, others more complete. This novel offers a refreshing view of one character's movement toward insight and integration in her life.

104 *Author:* Barker, Pat
Title: **Union Street** (1982). New York: Putnam, 1983
Genre: novel
Commentary: Each of the seven chapters in this novel recreates the experiences of a different woman who lives on Union Street, a lower-class area in an industrial city in the Midlands of England. Each chapter portrays the experiences of a woman older than the primary character in the previous chapter, so that the effect of the entire novel is a kind of intergenerational "stages of life" of all women on Union Street.

The experiences of the younger women provide a context for the crises that the older women face in later chapters. In the early chapters, the old are present either in memory or in the flesh to help the young face their problems and work toward a resolution of them. For example, after Kelly Brown, an adolescent girl, is raped in the first chapter, she experiences months of grief associated with this violent act. When she encounters an old woman in the park in the last chapter, she begins to resolve her pain by seeing her own old age in this old woman. Another young woman, who gives birth to her fourth child, at first does not accept her baby. But when she recalls her grandfather's response to his physical disability after a stroke, she is moved to begin to accept her new child. Another character works as a home health aide. She visits old people, and loves to "sit for hours listening to some old person's rambling memories of the past." Another woman, an old prostitute, interacts with a timid man, newly retired, and their encounter leaves him revitalized by the unpredictability of human experience.

The climactic last chapter features Alice Bell, an old woman who lives alone. Although her family has abandoned her, Alice's neighbors tend to her needs. But after a minor stroke, she is faced with the decision of moving into a convalescent hospital. Hobbled by the wreckage of her body and fearful of life in an institution, Alice commits herself to a personal "act of faith" and leaves her home. She finds her way to a park bench, where she interacts briefly with Kelly Brown: "The girl held out her hand. The withered hand and the strong young hand met and joined. . . . Then it was time for them both to go." The presence of the young girl is a fitting complement to Alice's story. Both characters experience different degrees of "violation," both know the feeling of being dispossessed, and both achieve a renewal of life based on their own efforts. Kelly is the child that Alice was; Alice is the old woman that Kelly will be. Their union echoes a comment by another character in an earlier chapter: "Every older woman became an image of the future, a reason for hope or fear."

The world of this novel is a woman's world, and the women in it are often trapped by poverty, by narrowly defined sex roles, by physical limitations, and by children who have lost a sense of filial piety. The old feel abandoned or displaced. But each chapter portrays the strength of character of the women, who either survive their personal ordeals or gain some measure of dignity in the attempt.

105 *Author:* Barker, Pat
   Title: **The Century's Daughter.** London: Putnam, 1986
   Genre: novel
   Commentary: Liza Jarrett, 84, lives an isolated existence in a run-down street in an urban center north of London. Into her world comes Stephen, a young social worker assigned to inform her that her house will be torn down as part of an urban renewal project. The friendship that develops between these two illustrates the power of intergenerational relationships to revive the later years. Their friendship offers resolutions for both characters: Liza helps Stephen recover feelings of love and grief toward his father, who dies in late middle age during the novel; and Stephen stimulates Liza to review her tragic life and recover loving memories of all of the men in her life.

Stephen's initial response to Liza is from the perspective of a detached professional. He does not look forward to the prospect of interacting with this uncouth old woman. But soon her honesty, wry humor, and insights into human interaction win him over. The two become friends. Stephen realizes that Liza is a person of strong character who has endured economic depressions, disabling family relationships, and the tragic deaths of her favorite brother and her only son in the two World Wars. As his fondness for Liza grows, Stephen works hard to help her survive in an increasingly hostile environment.

Born in 1900 (hence the title "The Century's Daughter"), Liza never escaped the poverty and despair of her working-class environment. She desperately loved her father, but he died when she was a young girl. Liza's mother never bonded with her daughter, and the two led an uneasy existence. Liza's husband, Frank, wounded in World War I, lost hope of becoming the breadwinner of the family during the Depression, and out of desperation he left her and their children. Now, like her mother, Liza is not close to her own daughter, Eileen. But when Eileen gives birth to a daughter out of wedlock, Liza raises the girl as if she were her own. Her granddaughter Kath becomes a replacement for all of the men she has lost in her life. Eventually claiming a victory over the cycles of poverty and oppression that have dominated her life, Liza sends Kath away to school at the end of the novel.

Liza feels a special closeness toward Stephen because he reminds her of her dead son. But Stephen's devotion to Liza cannot protect her from the brutality of alienated youths in the neighborhood. Liza dies after being beaten in a senseless robbery.

106 *Author:* Bausch, Richard
Title: **The Last Good Time.** Garden City, N.Y.: Doubleday, 1984
Genre: novel
Commentary: This novel is remarkable for its sympathetic vision of two lonely old widowers. Edward Cakes, a retired symphony violinist in his seventies, and his friend Arthur Hagood, a retired teacher aged 89, each have a "last good time" in a loving relationship, though their lives are generally bleak.

Edward is a mild man capable of anger and spunk. His worthless son, Ian, died in the Korean War; his wife, Ellen, soon after. His feeling for her is poeticized in his memory of a 1928 week-end with her in a Vermont cabin before their marriage; but he comes to realize, with pain, that he never really loved her enough. A young woman, Mary Bellini, stumbles into his flat, looking for the man who abandoned her. Edward befriends her, sleeps with her, and comes to love her (his "last good time"). Finally he discovers that Mary is a prostitute, hopelessly and cynically promiscuous, unable to value his affection. His last friendship, a minimal one, is with Ida Warren, a garrulous older woman who has moved in upstairs and dances endlessly to old records. At first bored by her, Edward comes at last to seek her out.

Arthur, whom Edward visits in the nursing home, still fantasizes about sex. He does recall a "last good time" with Maxine Sandusky when both were about 70. Edward brings him liquor and companionship until he dies in the home.

The smallest details are eloquent in this somber novel, and often the reader's mind lights up at some glowing sentence: "He [Edward] rose from the chair, his bones creaked, and the awareness of his age came to him like a rude remark."

107 *Author:* Bermant, Chaim
Title: **Diary of an Old Man.** New York: Holt, 1966
Genre: novel
Commentary: Cyril is an 84-year-old widower who lives alone in a small room in an apartment in a poor neighborhood in London. Cyril's diary offers a grim portrait of the loneliness, poverty, and isolation of the old. But this bleak vision is leavened by Cyril's acerbic wit, satiric views of his condition, and his sensitivity to the pathos in old people's lives.

Cyril leads a circumscribed life as a pensioner. He rarely goes outside his room, and a visit to the park seems a distant goal. He measures his life by the number of friends who have died before him. As he says, they "were carried off by one plague or another—mostly old age." Last year it was Dick, and the latest is Old Harry, who has just died when the novel begins.

The novel records Cyril's account of the events in his life from February 12 to March 15. In this month Cyril struggles against the cold (the heater in his room doesn't work); is hospitalized after falling asleep when he forgets to turn off the gas in his room; sees his one friend, George, almost every day; has many fond memories of his wife, who died when he was a young man; encounters a new tenant (a young black man studying for exams), and attempts to survive the harsh winter despite recurring episodes of dementia and worsening physical disabilities.

In early March, Cyril and George finally make their promised trip to the park for the first time in five months. There George collapses and dies, and Cyril is alone again. After his landlady is brutally murdered, he is forced to leave his building, and finally finds another room in a building owned by a friend of his former landlady. At the end of the novel, Cyril maintains an uneasy and meager existence.

108 *Author:* Berry, Wendell
Title: **The Memory of Old Jack.** New York: HBJ, 1974
Genre: novel
Commentary: Jack Beechum, born in 1860, reflects on his long life as a farmer in Kentucky. Now 92, Old Jack has a daily routine that consists of warming himself on the porch, stopping at the store to chat with friends, and eating his dinner in the dining room of a small hotel in town. The action in the present (1952) and in the past are a seamless whole through which Old Jack moves, spurred by sights and sounds around him. Each time he dips into the past, he reveals more of his character and relationships in earlier years. Eventually he is revealed as a complex character who made many mistakes in life but who learned to accept himself.

Old Jack recalls the influences that shaped his character, his love affair with the beautiful and mysterious Ruth, their marriage, the gradual disintegration of their relationship, an ill-fated extramarital affair, his struggles to escape debt, his starting life anew at the age of 48, and his wife's death when he was 75. At one point he admits that regret was "an emotion that would be one of the powerful themes of his life." Other themes are the need for the individual to respect the land and support the values of hard work, integrity, and resourcefulness; the continuity of generations of men who have worked the land; and the need to acknowledge and comprehend one's historical context.

In this regard Old Jack is characterized as a living monument, someone people look upon with awe and fondness, someone who reminds people of where they came from, what their lives mean, and where they are going. When he dies at the end of the story, his life is celebrated by the next-oldest man in town, his nephew, who will take Old Jack's place as a touchstone for future generations.

109 *Author:* Cary, Joyce
Title: **The Horse's Mouth.** London: Michael Joseph, 1944
Genre: novel
Commentary: Creativity in old age is the theme of this account of the disreputable artist Gulley Jimson in his final year. The never-

ending process of creativity itself is what Gulley keeps passionately talking about and practicing from the day he emerges from prison at age 67 to the day he is carried off to hospital with a stroke, as World War II breaks out.

Gulley is something of an Adam figure. He is the creator, the maker, the exploring man. He lives spontaneously, taking drink and sex with casual gusto, but art with unscrupulous intensity. To get himself time for painting or materials and money for it, Gulley will cheat, lie, steal, con, slug, betray with abandon. Although he has a hot temper and many opponents, he has no time for grudges or grievances; his sense of humor is wonderfully resilient.

His vagabondage includes a circle of original pals: Coker, a misanthropic barmaid furiously pregnant; Plant, a cobbler who studies philosophy; Nosy Barbon, a stuttering adolescent who worships Gulley as genius; his old mistress and model, Sara Monday. His major adventures include his invasion of his patrons' lodgings to set up a chaotic studio in their absence; his guiding a mob of art students as they paint the Creation on an abandoned wall.

The title of the novel is a racing term meaning that the betting tip has come from the highest authority, the horse itself. Here it refers to the direct intuition that Gulley receives from the heart of reality, the insight that generates his painting.

The Horse's Mouth is the third title of Cary's *First Trilogy,* each novel of which is the firsthand account of an older person living in the late 1930s. *Herself Surprised* (1941) is the reminiscence of Sara Monday, something of an Eve figure, a vulgar cheerful woman who has lived life to the hilt. *To Be a Pilgrim* (1942) is the life review of Thomas Whilcher, an anxious old gentleman who has never really learned to live. He is seen in his closing months as he tries to make sense of his own past and of the young generation represented by his unconventional niece. The three novels are independent of each other despite certain common characters. Although each complements the others in showing a range of attitudes toward life's adventures, *To Be a Pilgrim* might prove most taxing for the casual reader because of the density of its British historical background.

110   *Author:* Detre, Jean
      Title: **A Happy Ending.** New York: Simon & Schuster, 1967
      Genre: novel
      Commentary: The relationship between an old man and his live-in companion, a middle-aged woman, grows beyond the bounds of a professional relationship as the two forge a warm friendship and

eventually the stronger bonds of love. As their affection toward each other grows, they discover unexplored dimensions in their characters and achieve important personal goals.

Isadore Rose, 79, a widower and a millionaire, lives in dull, uninspired retirement in Clearwater, Florida. He has suffered a mild stroke. To aid his convalescence, his sister-in-law hires a live-in companion, Mrs. Sweet-William. She is 40, widowed for seven years. Before long, Mr. Rose frees himself from the cautions of his doctors, the constraints of family ties, and the demands of university fund raisers by deciding on the spur of the moment to tour the Continent. Aided by Mrs. Sweet-William, Mr. Rose journeys to Italy and to the Holy Land.

Mrs. Sweet-William remains in the background, always dutiful, but never too solicitous. She is an engaging character who becomes devoted to the needs of her employer. In time they become close friends. Eventually Mr. Rose proposes marriage, specifically because he wishes to recognize the quality of companionship that exists between them. Although she refuses his offer, Mrs. Sweet-William stays with him so that he can complete his journey to the Holy Land in search of an ultimate meaning for his life.

Mr. Rose dies in Jordan before they complete their journey. The circumstances surrounding his death are bizarre; his body mysteriously disappears after his death, and despite Mrs. Sweet-William's frantic attempts to resolve the mystery, his body is never found. But events in the novel suggest that before his death Mr. Rose found the meaning he had sought on his journey: he gained a measure of personal happinesss and control over his life by freeing himself from all that was expected of him by family and society.

Further evidence of his personal growth is provided when Mrs. Sweet-William is named as the sole beneficiary of Mr. Rose's will. This turn of events aids Mrs. Sweet-William's growth of character as well. She realizes his gift acknowledges the bond between them. She knows that his decision will be contested and that she will be forced to defend her claim. But she accepts that responsibility as a final act of devotion to her former employer.

111 *Author:* Edgerton, Clyde
Title: **Walking Across Egypt** (1987). New York: Ballantine, 1988
Genre: novel
Commentary: In this comic novel, an elderly widow combines her culinary talents, her faith, and her social and interpersonal skills to redeem the life of a wayward youth. Mattie Rigsbee, 78, lives alone

in a small town in North Carolina. She is a practical, self-reliant, devout Christian. But her true calling, or vocation, is cooking for people. Throughout the novel, people are attracted to her because of her delicious Southern cooking and her willingness to listen to people's stories without being judgmental.

Her family and neighbors would prefer that Mattie act like an old woman—passive and dependent. They are frustrated by her trusting, open ways with strangers. But Mattie survives their stereotyping and thrives on her interactions with the assorted characters who are drawn to her bountiful table. Her only regret is that her two children have never married. Thus she has no grandchildren.

Mattie tries to live her life according to her religion. She takes seriously Jesus's admonition that "Whatso ye do unto one of the least of these my brethren you do also to me." She has an opportunity to act upon those words when she meets a juvenile delinquent who has been jailed for stealing a car. At first she visits the young man out of a sense of duty. In time the young man begins to be influenced by her honesty and compassion. Mattie realizes that God has answered her prayers and that she can experience grandparenthood vicariously if she takes in this young man. She agrees to become his legal guardian.

Every night Mattie sits at her piano and plays hymns. Her favorite hymn is "Walking Across Egypt." One line of the hymn reads, "My faith is set before me and my journey shall be blest." Mattie acts on her faith in her relationships with everyone in the novel. She is a modern-day Moses who leads a downtrodden and weary young man toward the promised land of self-respect, freedom, and family ties.

112 *Author:* Gaines, Ernest J.
   Title: **The Autobiography of Miss Jane Pittman.** New York: Dial, 1971
   Genre: novel
   Commentary: This novel is structured as an oral history of Miss Jane Pittman, a former slave who lived more than a hundred years and witnessed the beginnings of the Civil Rights movement in the South. The narrative recreates the old woman's reminiscences of her childhood, marriage, and middle age. Miss Jane's tenacity, faith in the land, and dedication to her loved ones are her essential traits. Her story is a painful testimony to the injustices faced by black people throughout American history. Her strength of character, and especially her equanimity in the face of bigotry, will inspire readers.

The first half of the book contains the finest part of her story. Miss Jane speaks directly to the reader, recalling her childhood days as a newly freed slave, and her departure from the plantation with many adults who sought to find a new life. When a band of renegades massacres the adults one night in a barn, Miss Jane escapes with a younger boy, Ned, the son of Big Laura, the leader of the group. Her adventures continue as she and Ned try to return to Ohio, the home of a soldier who gave the slave girl Ticey the name "Jane."

Miss Jane never reaches Ohio, although she does live in Texas with her husband, Joe Pittman, before he dies tragically; and her precious Ned is murdered by whites when he refuses to stop preaching a gospel of black pride to his people. Her sense of self deepened by these tragedies, Miss Jane spends the rest of her life in the old slave quarters she came to after Joe Pittman died.

113 *Author:* Gloag, Julian
Title: **Only Yesterday.** New York: Henry Holt, 1986
Genre: novel
Commentary: Oliver Darley, a retired architect, lives with his wife, May, in their London home, which is in a state of general disrepair. One day their middle-aged son, Rupert, who has left his second wife and left his teaching job, turns up on their doorstep. The next day his daughter Miranda, a pre-med student, arrives for a planned visit. As the weekend unfolds, the members of this family learn to adapt to each other's needs, resolve some immediate and long-term personal crises, and renew the bonds of their personal relationships. Although the new ideas of Rupert and Miranda often meet resistance and delay, the old couple gradually adapts to their helpful presence, and before the end of the novel the old couple share revealing secrets from their pasts that provide some insight into the development of their characters and values.

Although Rupert seems to lack a clear direction to his life because of recent events, he uses his stay with his parents as an opportunity to restore his self-esteem and to renew his relationship with his parents and with his daughter. Rupert assists his parents with housekeeping chores, supports May's request to enter the hospital for therapy, volunteers to stay with Oliver while May is there, and then decides to stay on with May after Oliver dies suddenly of a heart attack.

Gloag captures the nuances and routines that have shaped the patterns of behavior of the elderly couple. Oliver is deftly portrayed as an old curmudgeon, often irascible, impatient, and angry about the physical losses related to aging. May is frustrated with the physical pain and limitations associated with her disabilities. She is weary of Oliver's resistance to change, yet she remains devoted to him.

114 *Author:* Hemingway, Ernest
   Title: **The Old Man and the Sea.** New York: Scribner, 1952
   Genre: novel
   Commentary: On a literal level, this novel is a fine adventure story of an old Cuban fisherman who rows far out to sea and hooks a great marlin that he tries to bring back. In the fisherman, Santiago, Hemingway also embodies a stoic outlook by which to endure and conquer all that would crush humanity—especially old age and hostile nature.

   Santiago has not brought in a marketable big fish for eighty-four days. Though once a formidable man, he is now old, he is a widower, he is essentially a loner. On this day he rows out beyond the usual fishing waters, hooks the great fish, and engages in an epic struggle as the fish runs deep and fast, pulling Santiago's skiff hour after hour, into night and another day and still another night and day. The old man copes with all his strength and cunning, doing wonders in his pain and exhaustion. At last he subdues the greatest fish of his experience, so big that he cannot bring it aboard but must lash it to the side of the skiff. The sharks move in. By the time he reaches shore, the sharks have devoured all the fish but head and skeleton. The old man, both winner and loser, stumbles home to his shack and sleep.

   Although Santiago might be thought of as a simple man, he is thoughtful, even poetic in his sense of comradeship with the great fish, the wandering warbler bird, the porpoises, even the stars. As long as he has any weapon to his hand, he fights off the marauding sharks that, like old age, tear away at his achievement.

   A softening element in Santiago's bleak old age is the admiring affection of the young boy, Manolin, who takes almost parental care of his friend and who at the end vows to join Santiago as apprentice even though the old man's health may have broken.

115 *Author:* Laurence, Margaret
   Title: **The Stone Angel.** New York: Knopf, 1964
   Genre: novel
   Commentary: Hagar Shipley is a woman of 90 who lives in her son's home and pleases no one, including herself. In this novel we follow

her reminiscences of growing up in a small Canadian town. Her mother died giving birth to her, and that is the source for the "stone angel," a monument to her mother. Hagar married the man her father did not want her to marry and raised two sons, one of whom could do no wrong in her mind. At the end of her life she discovers how much happiness and self-fulfilment she has lost because of the unforgiving force of her character.

Hagar is a well-individuated character, whose first-person narrative is at once honest, unyielding, and tragic. Her life review draws readers into her most painful memory—the death of her favorite son. We see a woman, already blinded by motherly love, turned into "stone" by grief. The headnote of the book is an excerpt from the Dylan Thomas poem, "Do Not Go Gentle into That Good Night." Hagar never ceases raging "against the light."

Hagar's caregivers are her son, Marvin, and his wife, Doris. Although both mean well in their interactions with Hagar, their ministrations often fall short when they come up against Hagar's abrasive character. She shows little affection towards either of them and resents their plan to have her placed in a nursing home. One day Hagar leaves home, without telling them, to revisit a significant place from her past. In this scene, and in other scenes later when she is in a hospital, Hagar connects with strangers who in small but meaningful ways help her gain some sense of closure with her life before she dies.

116   *Author:* Lawrence, Josephine
      Title: **Years Are So Long.** New York: Grosset, 1934
      Genre: novel
      Commentary: When Barkley Cooper, 73, is forced to retire, he expects that his wife and he will be accepted into the home of one of their five children to live out their days in security and peace. But their children refuse to accept what they consider to be an undue burden of caregiving. The old couple are forced to live separately in their children's homes on a rotating basis. But this arrangement leads to the parent's emotional and physical decline. When Barkley dies after a brief illness, the family meets to decide the mother's fate. They decide to place her, against her will, in an "Old Ladies' Home."

The old couple faces common challenges as they adjust to living apart from each other in their children's homes: both feel alienated, rejected, and ignored by their children; both are overwhelmed by generational differences; both find friendship and acceptance only from others who lack power and influence; both try repeatedly to escape from their hostile environments; and both fail to escape their unhappy living arrangements because they experience feelings of low self-esteem, insecurity, and debilitating fears of poverty and physical decline.

No one in the family seems to have time for the parents. One couple works constantly to make ends meet. Another is obsessed with paying for an annuity so that they will have sufficient retirement income. The marriages of the other two children are failing. The children all view their parents with ageist stereotypes: that the old couple are old-fashioned, out of touch with current events, and incapable of understanding their children's particular problems.

The children's negative, even hostile attitudes toward aging underscore the didactic nature of this tale. If Barkley and Lucy had had access to Social Security (the Townsend Amendment was passed in 1934), they might have been able to afford to live together and preserve some measure of dignity and self-respect.

117   *Author:* Lawrence, Josephine
      Title: **The Web of Time.** New York: Harcourt, 1953
      Genre: novel
      Commentary: This novel pleads against the concept of mandatory retirement. It is still timely even though the laws have been relaxed since the 1950s. It carries a cumulative journalistic force in the vein of Sinclair Lewis, to present an excellent case study on the retirement problems of simple people.

Munsey Wills, a complaint-department clerk for a mail order house, at age 65 undergoes mandatory retirement for which he is in no way fitted. His job has been his life, his narcotic, just as keeping house has been for his wife Jennie. "If people want to work," he says, "seems to me they ought to be allowed. 'Tisn't so much the money—it's keeping busy at what you like to do."

In the following two years of painful idleness, Munsey finds little better to do than to stay out of his wife's way and then to insist on adopting a dog (a lifelong wish). He finds part-time employment at last as a museum guard and recovers some balance of spirit. His quiet suffering has been intensified by the mistaken notion of others that what he wants is either Florida or a hobby. His daughter, Kew, continues to make selfish demands. His wife bitterly resents having to leave her home routine to earn money as a store clerk.

Ultimately the novel presents Munsey's failure to live well and hence to age well. "Had it been a mistake, he wondered now, to let the office fill in the disappointments, the unanswered yearnings, that he had been unwilling to examine or to try to understand? Work had been his antidote for everything he had missed, but would it have been wiser to have faced the emptiness and explored it, rather than to have chosen an opiate?"

118 *Author:* Mason, Bobbie Ann
Title: **Spence + Lila.** New York: Harper, 1988
Genre: novel
Commentary: An old couple face one of the greatest challenges of their life when the wife is diagnosed as having cancer of the breast. Spence and Lila, who own a small farm near Paducah, Kentucky, have been married for forty years. In this crisis the character of the two old people and the strong bonds of their relationship are revealed through their interactions with each other and with their three adult children. When Spence and Lila are alone, their memories of their early relationship sustain them. Their simple faith in each other and in the land they work help them persevere. Although their lives may be considered ordinary, their honesty, openness, and strong values illustrate how beautiful a "normal" or ordinary life can be.

Spence worries that Lila will die after one of her surgeries, and he is concerned that he will not be able to deal with life without Lila. But Spence's concerns are never the source of an overly sentimental response to life. Spence and Lila have preserved an innocence about themselves. They are old, but they are not jaded, cynical, or troubled with regrets. They live their lives day to day, unconcerned with deep philosophical questions. They don't reflect on the meaning of their relationship or the meaning of their old age. They have few second thoughts about how they have lived their lives. They distrust grand shows of feelings. Instead, they simply engage life as an ongoing and welcome challenge.

Their family rallies around them in Lila's illness. This family has no dark secrets or unresolved pains. The children are functional adults who face this disruption in their lives together. Lila admits one thing she has learned from these events: "You think your family takes you for granted and then you find out they care a whole lot more than you thought they did."

The author writes the title with a plus sign rather than using the word *and* because these two people are bonded in the deepest sense through their marriage. They have joined identities to form that union. They are devoted to each other.

119 *Author:* Naipaul, V. S.
   Title: **Mrs. Stone and the Knights Companion** (1963). New York: Macmillan, 1964
   Genre: novel
   Commentary: This short novel moves quietly, seamlessly through the many small events of Richard Stone's life as he comes to see himself: "a gentle, endearing man nearing retirement, of no particular consequence." With affection, Naipaul shows the pathos of aging for solitary gentle people; the sometimes wan chances of later marriage; the thin possibilities of friendship with the young.

   Aged 62, Mr. Stone is a white-collar London bachelor, timid, with few friends in or out of his office. His witty account of his vendetta with a neighboring cat draws the admiring attention of Margaret Springer, a fiftyish widow. They wed and gradually "become married" though to the reader they still seem strangers to each other.

   Mr. Stone's big event—and unexpected success—is his brainstorm for a project later designated as the Knights Companion, whereby the retirees of his firm will visit the retirees of client firms to spread good will and note special needs. The firm picks up the idea and assigns its public relations person to promote it, which is done to hilarious excess. Stone is catapulted into small celebrity that climaxes at a dinner party where all seems right.

   Stone's modest renewal soon fades. The PR specialist turns his attention elsewhere. Stone's impending retirement dims his brief importance at the office. In a final walk home to a darkened house, Stone elegiacally considers the alien quality of the universe and the destructiveness of human nature but he ends with the weary confidence that his own serenity will return.

120 *Author:* Nathan, Robert
   Title: **The Color of Evening.** New York: Knopf, 1960
   Genre: novel
   Commentary: By giving up his dream of a May–December love affair with a young woman he befriends and shelters, Max Loeb, an aging portrait artist, learns to accept his old age, to find compensations in life for what was lost or never acquired, and to help others who are just beginning to face the complicated struggles required by life. At the same time, Max resolves his own loneliness and anxiety by accepting the risks attendant in a new relationship with a woman his age.

Max Loeb, who has never married, lives alone in an elderly widow's garage in Santa Monica. Max has lost inspiration for his art, and he has become fearful of physical decline. He is articulate, well-educated and has an opinion on most subjects. He is reasonably happy in his semi-retirement. He sells an occasional portrait, and he earns a modest income tutoring an art student, John Kuzik, with whom he has developed a close friendship. Max's landlady, Mrs. Bloemendahl, has long regarded him with affection. But he views her as a distant, remote figure, someone who is too sure in her faith and who doesn't understand his philosophical musings about life.

Max's comfortable life is upset when John and he find Halys Smith, a young drifter from Oregon, passed out on the beach one night. Max takes her in and she recovers her strength. Against his better judgment, Max falls in love with the young woman. Meanwhile, she has fallen desperately in love with John. Eventually the two young people run away to Mexico to get married. Max is devastated by this loss. But after several months the young couple's idyllic relationship sours when faced with the realities of rent payments and housekeeping duties.

Halys, confused and unsure of her motives, returns to Max's home and offers to live with him if he wants her to. But Max realizes that she still loves John and that the young couple's marriage may survive if they are given another opportunity to live together. He also realizes that he has begun to fall in love with Mrs. Bloemendahl. Max has been moved by her kindness, which gave her "a sort of beauty. A woman like that, he thought, does not need any security from me, she has her own." So Max suggests that Halys and John move into the garage while Max takes a room in Mrs. Bloemendahl's house. His plan works well for everyone involved. Halys and John are reunited, and Max begins a new life with Mrs. Bloemendahl.

121 *Author:* O'Connor, Edwin
Title: **I Was Dancing**. New York: Little, 1964
Genre: novel
Commentary: One year ago Daniel Considine (always referred to as "Old Daniel" in the text) suddenly showed up on his son Tom's doorstep after an absence of twenty years. Where has he been? His only answer is, "I was dancing." Daniel is a master of self-deception who dresses up the truth of his past and ignores the fact that he left his wife when Tom was a boy, returned only for his wife's funeral twenty years ago, and then left his son again. The novel illustrates

the son's struggle to resist his father's appealing version of the story of his life and rid himself of an old man who is practically a stranger to him and in all respects an intruder in his own home. Their intergenerational relationship is a reminder that not all father-son conflicts can be resolved. Despite the idealized image of the "father" as a kindly, loving figure (an image deeply embedded in our culture), the reality of *this* father is that of a self-centered, vindictive old man who responded to family responsibilities with indifference and neglect.

In the past year Old Daniel has lived in an upstairs room of his son's house. The story begins a month after Tom and his wife, frustrated with hearing the old man's endless stories about his days as a dancer in vaudeville, ask Daniel to move to a retirement center. Out of spite old Daniel has not spoken to them for the entire month. Old Daniel, the "prodigal father," is determined to remain an unwanted guest in his son's home.

Tom would like to see their relationship reconciled. After all, Old Daniel still is Tom's father, and Tom fears abandoning him altogether. But one of Tom's colleagues, who is estranged from his own father, advises Tom, "You know what your trouble is? You have no experience: you've never thrown your father out before." In the climactic scene Old Daniel plays the role of the kind, helpless father, but his act fails to convince Tom, who is prepared to defy his father's clever tricks. Realizing that his plan has been foiled, Old Daniel reveals his pent-up vindictiveness, pettiness, and hatred toward his son before he leaves.

122	*Author:* Pym, Barbara
Title: **Quartet in Autumn.** New York: Dutton, 1978
Genre: novel
Commentary: The "Quartet" of the title refers to Marcia, Norman, Edwin, and Letty, all in their sixties, clerical workers in a London office. They participate in the expected gossip and banter of people who work together, and yet they know almost nothing about their colleagues' personal lives. Pym's novel is a bleak vision of old age as a time of loneliness and missed opportunities. These four old people do not connect; they retreat behind dull routines, idiosyncratic behaviors, and the fear of revealing intimate details of their lives. Within this framework, however, Pym suggests that those older people who engage life directly and openly have the greatest opportunity for growth and self-development.

At first glance, all of the characters, who live alone, seem incapable of sustained change and growth. Marcia, who never married, is "ageing, slightly mad, and approaching the threshold of retirement." She is an incurably private person who never recovered from the death of her mother. She exhibits strange behaviors (hoarding cans of food and empty milk bottles) that allow her to feel some measure of control over her environment. A young social worker aide visits her regularly, but Marcia considers these visits intrusions and rejects her offers of aid. After her retirement she becomes reclusive, physically frail, increasingly demented, and she finally dies of cancer.

Norman is an angry old man who appears to be dissatisfied with life. He feels most comfortable when he is at work in the office, and he even spends part of his holidays there. Often he makes uncouth and inappropriate remarks. After Marcia dies, he is surprised to learn that Marcia has willed her home to him.

Edwin is a conservative, high-church Anglican who spends most of his time observing the various Saints' Days in the church calendar. A widower, he has the clearest "role" of the four, as father and grandfather.

Of the four, Letty stands out as the one character most capable of personal growth. Letty's options in life seem to narrow early in the novel. Her plans to move to the country and live with a close friend, Marjorie, are disrupted when the latter, a widow, decides to remarry. Then Letty's landlady sells her house to a man who insists on holding noisy religious services in the house. Although she feels daunted by this turn of events, she survives a move to a different apartment, and after her retirement adjusts to new routines. When Marjorie's marriage plans are dashed by her suitor, Majorie expects Letty to live with her as before. But now Letty postpones making that decision. She realizes she has choices in life.

123 *Author:* Sackville-West, Victoria
Title: **All Passion Spent.** Garden City, N.Y.: Doubleday, 1931
Genre: novel
Commentary: Besides showing the power of life review and integration in late life, this novel contains eloquent passages on the role of women, on the physical and psychological changes of old age. An 88-year-old widow looks back and recovers the real self that she had buried in a lifetime as dutiful wife of a distinguished English public leader.

Deborah Holland, Lady Slane, determines on the death of her
husband Lord Henry to live alone in a quiet London suburb despite
the objections of her snobbish, already elderly children who expect
her to continue as a public figure. She finds simple companionship
with her old, faithful maid, Genoux; her philosophical landlord,
Mr. Bucktrout; and a sensible tradesman, Mr. Gosheron. As the serene days pass, Lady Slane reflects on her life as consort to Henry
Holland, viceroy to India and later prime minister, a greatly gifted
diplomat, impeccably charming and considerate—but at the heart,
cold. Young Deborah had wanted ardently to become an artist, a
painter. But she succumbed to the conspiracy whereby Victorian
men and women alike expected a lady to serve her husband, to be
his extension and comfort. So Deborah had lived out her "duty,"
loyal to Henry, loving him in a conventional way, with her secret self
in abeyance.

But another man appears at her door—FitzGeorge, an eccentric
old millionaire art collector who, as it turns out, she had met long
ago in India when both were young. He had seen through her
façade, to the wild spirit behind, and had fallen in love for the only
time in his reclusive life. The remainder of the novel shows Deborah's awakening to his recall; their quiet but rich friendship on the
threshold of the death that overtakes them both; and the passing of
her new freedom to her great-granddaughter Deborah, almost
caught in the same web.

124 *Author:* Sarton, May
Title: **As We Are Now.** New York: Norton, 1973
Genre: novel
Commentary: "I am not mad, only old. I make this statement to
give me courage. To give you an idea what I mean by courage, suf-
fice it to say that it has taken two weeks for me to obtain this note-
book and a pen. I am in a concentration camp for the old, a place
where people dump their parents or relatives exactly as though it
were an ash can."

With this opening, Caro Spencer—76, single, fiercely independent, a former math teacher with a love of poetry—tells of her stay
at Twin Elms, a substandard nursing home in the countryside. Her
"keeper" is Harriet Hatfield, a mean and vindictive woman who
makes this place a nasty inferno. The other inmates are Standish
Flint, a bitter but dignified farmer close to death, and several senile
men.

Twin Elms is indeed a cautionary showcase of elderly abuse both physical and mental, and merits attention for that reason alone. Caro tries to save both her sanity and her soul in struggling against it. She finds moral support in Richard Thornhill, a sensitive minister, and affection in Anna Close, a farmer's wife who comes in as substitute attendant. But the battle is a losing one, reversed only by Caro's climatic act of purgative rage in which she destroys Twin Elms by fire.

Sarton's writing coruscates with insights into aging: "Old age is really a disguise that no one but the old themselves see through." "Old age is not interesting until one gets there, a foreign country with an unknown language to the young, and even to the middle-aged." Her title here is ominously relevant, coming from a New England tombstone epitaph: "As you are now, so once was I; Prepare for death and follow me."

This excellent brief novel may lead the reader into Sarton's other works on aging: novels such as *A Reckoning* or autobiography in *At Seventy* (entry 514) or in much of her poetry (as introduced in entry 430).

125 *Author:* Spark, Muriel
   Title: **Memento Mori.** Philadelphia: Lippincott, 1959
   Genre: novel
   Commentary: This novel is an eloquent reminder of the follies that can pursue people into the late years and of the need to put one's life in order. Anonymous telephone calls tell the various characters, "Remember you must die"—the traditional religious admonishment to consider last things. (The title is Latin for that message.) The setting is London. The time is the 1950s.

But most of these people—upper middle-class British intellectuals—continue to live as spitefully, haughtily, greedily, noisily, lustfully, self-absorbedly as they did in their prime early in the century. Only two or three have used old age as a time for fruitful reflection on their mortality.

This macabre comedy exposes a gallery of aged reprobates: Dame Lettie Colston, who tries to dominate others by the constant remaking of her will; Godfrey Colston, overshadowed by his wife Charmian's fame as a novelist, who has conducted numerous affairs and now settles for a glimpse of a lady's garter; Mabel Pettigrew, lady's companion who blackmails and intrigues to improve her wealth and station; Percy Mannering, the superannuated poet who can write sonnets about death as a mere prosodic exercise. Perhaps the most comic of all is Alec Warner, the amateur gerontologist who seeks to study the crises of old age by taking pulse and temperature.

The most serious character seems to be Henry Mortimer, retired chief inspector who can say: "If I had my life over again I should form the habit of nightly composing myself to thoughts of death. I would practise, as it were, the remembrance of death. There is no other practise which so intensifies life. Death, when it approaches, ought not to take one by surprise. It should be part of the full expectancy of life. Without an ever-present sense of death life is insipid." And there is Jean Taylor, former lady's companion, who says things like: "Being over seventy is like being engaged in a war. All our friends are going or gone and we survive amongst the dead and the dying as on a battlefield." Or, "How nerve-wracking it is to be getting old, how much better to be old!"

126 *Author:* Stegner, Wallace
Title: **The Spectator Bird.** New York: Doubleday, 1976
Genre: novel
Commentary: Joe Allston, 69, is a retired literary agent who lives with his wife, Ruth, in the San Francisco Bay area of California in 1974. Throughout the novel he rages at the physical changes of his aging body, the prospects for further physical decline, and the ageism he perceives in society's rejection of the old. Joe and Ruth retired to California to find their "safe place," but Joe still feels vulnerable, alienated, and alone in a dangerous world. Stegner portrays old age unflinchingly as a time of anxiety and uncertainty, but he suggests that the best antidote to the condition of old age is to find someone with whom to share its attendant pain and alienation.

Joe's pain extends to two events from the past that still haunt him. He has never recovered from the shock of his only son's death by drowning more than twenty years earlier, because he is not convinced the death was accidental. He also has never resolved his feelings about a mysterious woman, Astrid, whom Ruth and he met on a trip to Denmark after his son died.

Memories of this fateful trip resurface when Joe and Ruth receive a postcard from Astrid. Joe retrieves from his files notebooks he completed on the Denmark trip. Ruth, who prefers to manage conflict by confronting and overcoming the worst in a crisis, persuades him to begin reading the notebooks aloud each evening, and the novel moves back and forth between the narrative recorded in his notebooks and the narrative in the present.

Joe and Ruth become Astrid's friends and protectors. She is a beautiful and mysterious woman. But after she takes Joe and Ruth to visit her family's estate, Joe begins to unravel several dark secrets. He learns that Astrid's father, a famous geneticist, began human experiments to test his theories by impregnating more than one generation of servant girls. He also learns that Astrid's brother has continued the experiment with descendants of those children.

Although the recollection of these discoveries is a devastating emotional blow to both Joe and Ruth, for Ruth another unresolved matter needs to be aired. She has been waiting for Joe to address his relationship to Astrid. But Joe did not record a climactic encounter between Astrid and himself near the end of their trip. When Ruth presses him to reveal his feelings for Astrid, he suffers an emotional crisis, runs out of the house, and relives the evening spent twenty years ago when he spent several hours alone with Astrid. What happened? Their encounter was magical, and it was climaxed with a passionate kiss. Then they parted. Nothing more occurred between them. But Joe has kept secret this encounter for twenty years. The novel ends when Ruth joins Joe outside and helps him begin to restore his self-confidence and self-esteem after facing these ghosts from his past.

127 *Author:* Taylor, Elizabeth
Title: **Mrs. Palfrey at the Claremont.** New York: Viking, 1971
Genre: novel
Commentary: The brave boredom of being old in a retirement hotel is described in this study of Laura Palfrey, widow of a British Empire civil servant. On a rainy January day she comes to the Claremont Hotel, residence of a few old ladies and an occasional gentleman, who will linger here until disability pushes them on to nursing homes or geriatric wards. The routine is deadly: inspecting the day's menus, dawdling until dinner, knitting, television, shopping errands. One constantly checks the passing of time by one's watch, to find as Mrs. Palfrey does, that "it was always earlier than she thought it would be."

Elizabeth Taylor creates in this motley crowd a rare and sometimes comic gallery of retirees meeting old age with a wide range of pluck and resourcefulness. Elvira Arbuthnot rages against age with a spiteful tongue discharged on the others. Mrs. Post meets the smallest incident with lugubrious timidity. Mrs. Burton drinks. Mr. Osmond, for a time the sole man, combines a disdainful aloofness with a pathetic desire for rapport with the male staff. And so on.

What sets Mrs. Palfrey apart is a stoic dignity combined with the considerateness of an old-fashioned lady. She has resolved to "soldier on," as her husband would have had her do, following three simple rules: "Be independent; never give way to melancholy; never touch capital."

In the main action of the novel, Mrs. Palfrey develops a restrained friendship with Ludo, a hungry young writer who helps her recover from a bad fall on the street. At the Claremont she proudly passes him off as her grandson (the real one had never called). Ludo plays up to the grandson role with sympathetic wit. In his turn he takes notes, to use as a writer, on her and the Claremont. Though Mrs. Palfrey rightly expects little from this otherwise preoccupied young man, he means so much to her that she breaks a rule by dipping into capital to help him. After she suffers another fall, he repays both her affection and her money as he visits her deathbed. In a second action, Mrs. Palfrey accepts the respectful attentions of the lonely Mr. Osmond but declines his offer of marriage: "I had one perfect marriage. That suffices."

128 *Author:* Trevor, William
Title: **The Old Boys.** New York: Viking, 1964
Genre: novel
Commentary: Failed dreams and bitter memories of unhappy childhoods collide in this story about the machinations of a number of alumni from one of England's public schools. The "old boys," all between 70 and 75, are members of a committee of the "Old Boy's Association." They meet a few times a year "to discuss this and that" and to reminisce about their school days. For most of the characters their school days were the high point of their lives. Their old age is spent in idle chatter, trivial pursuits, and dull routines. As one of the characters notes, "We are bystanders, as befits people of our age." Their attempts to infuse their lives with drama often appear slightly absurd, if not pathetic.

Their common bond—having attended the same school—is a source of pleasure to some of the old boys and a source of pain to others. One of the old boys in particular strives to recapture what he considers to be the glorious days of childhood. Jaraby is an ill-humored and self-centered old man who is obsessed with becoming the next president of the committee. His years in school taught him that boys are made strong and whole by learning to "take it"—that is, by being harassed and brutalized at every opportunity. In his years as "Head of the House" he treated his younger charges according to that formula.

Now Jaraby faces two formidable foes who are bent on blocking his rush to glory: his wife, who plans to welcome their estranged son back into their home despite Jaraby's objections, and Nox, who was one of the students in Jaraby's House. In school Jaraby treated Nox with particular cruelty because Nox would not learn to "take it." Nox has always resented this brutality, and now he sees an opportunity to block Jaraby's goal and exact revenge. The machinations of Jaraby's two adversaries eventually lead to Jaraby's downfall.

129 *Author:* Updike, John
Title: **The Poorhouse Fair.** New York: Knopf, 1958
Genre: novel
Commentary: A number of old men and women lead a dreary existence in the Diamond County Home for the Aged in central New Jersey, an institution better known as the "poorhouse" by local people. For these people old age is a time of helplessness, insecurity, and—worst of all—boredom. To make matters worse, the people who are responsible for their care patronize the old people and control their lives rigidly and unfeelingly.

John F. Hook, 84, a former schoolteacher, is the resident philosopher of the Home and a spokesperson for the other residents. Bill Gregg, 70, is an angry old man whose speech is sprinkled with four-letter words and who strikes out wherever possible—often blindly—when he is subjected to injustice. Conner, the prefect (administrator), regards old age with distaste. He reluctantly mingles with the old people, and he dreams of gaining a better position someday. To Connor, old people are impediments to progress. They resist change; they live in the past. Conner distrusts Hook because he considers the old man to be a threat to his authority.

On this day the residents are preparing to brighten their otherwise dull routine by organizing the annual fair. People from nearby towns are to mingle on the grounds, purchase handmade wares, and renew old acquaintances. Because of a rain shower, the fair is delayed until the afternoon. Meanwhile, Conner's patronizing attitude toward the residents precipitates a spontaneous physical attack on him in the climactic scene of the novel. Conner asks the residents to help him repair a damaged stone wall. Spurred on by Gregg, the residents throw stones at Conner until he runs away. Although he is unhurt, Conner is overwhelmed by the depth of their rage and he responds with petty vindictiveness.

The fair is held in the afternoon. Unfortunately, the townspeople who attend care little for the individual fates of the old people who live in the institution. "They felt the poorhouse would always be there, exempt from time." The visitors respond to their own private agendas, and when the fair is over they return to their homes untouched by their interactions with the old people. The old people, in their turn, resume the routines that had consumed them before the fair began.

130   *Author:* Van Velde, Jacoba
      Title: **The Big Ward.** Trans. by Ellen and Roy Hulbert. New York: Simon & Schuster, 1960
      Genre: novel
      Commentary: The drama of life in a public assistance ward of a Dutch nursing home is the focus of this novel. The symbol of the big ward dominates the novel. In this ward the most seriously incapacitated residents go to die. It is an impersonal place lacking privacy and individuality, where the moans of dying patients are heard day and night. The big ward is the ultimate symbol of society's tendency to discard the old. It also represents the old person's fear of the unknown, ultimately the fear of death.

The events of the novel are told in the alternating first-person accounts of Trudi Van der Veen, 74, and her daughter, Helena. Trudi wakes up one morning to discover that she has been in the nursing home for four days after suffering a stroke. Now her struggle becomes how to avoid being moved into the big ward. Although Trudi and the other old women in the nursing home experience tensions, fears, and recurring feelings of helplessness and despair, they survive because of their empathy toward each other. They listen to each other's stories, and they share their private griefs. The caregivers in the nursing home are portrayed as sensitive persons who are often overwhelmed by the magnitude of the task of caring for these old people.

Helena's affection for her mother is evident. She is deeply committed to her mother's care. Helena's status as caregiver is complicated by several factors. She is expected by law to pay for her mothers' care; but she is unable to contribute much because her husband and she do not have regular incomes. She lives in Paris and her mother is in Holland. She hates to see her mother in the nursing home, but she is powerless to change the circumstances of her mother's situation. Despite these constraints, Helena perseveres. She visits her mother regularly, she takes her on an outing two days before she has to return to Paris, and she is at her mother's side when she dies.

131 *Author:* Wharton, William (pseudonym)
Title: **Dad.** New York: Knopf, 1981
Genre: novel
Commentary: John Tremont, a fiftyish painter, tries to see his Dad through an ultimate crisis of health, self-acceptance, and marriage, at the same time that he tries to cope with his own life and son.

Place and time: Los Angeles, about 1977. Called home from Paris by his mother's heart attack, John finds an equal crisis in Dad, John Sr., aged 73. An intelligent blue-collar craftsman retired from Douglas Aircraft, Dad is timid, dominated by Mom, a bigoted insecure woman who manipulates all those around her. After an operation for bladder cancer, Dad goes through extreme stages of infantile withdrawal, rejuvenating recovery into the lively full-spirited man he might have been, submergence in a fantasy rustic life (which he has secretly cherished for many years). Owing largely to Mom's frantic hostility, Dad finally withdraws again and dies in a nursing home.

The major theme is the son's caring: "Why is it I had to wait so long to know my dad is a man like myself, more like me than anybody I've ever met. . . . We have, in our deepest selves, beyond the masks of time and experience, a communal identity. What is it that keeps fathers and sons so far apart?"

Other themes are: the need for militant opposition to bureaucratic medical authority; the possibilities of imaginative doctoring and nursing; the possible recovery in old age of latent potential for living; the surfacing in old age of spousal fears and hostilities.

The son's first-person narrative alternates with narrative by *his* son Bill, a hippy drop-out who comes closer to his father as the two drive East after leaving Dad in his terminal illness (where the novel opens). Italicized interludes convey the secret fantasy life lived by Dad, who in a sense harks back to the idyllic farm life of his boyhood home in Wisconsin.

Whether any one old person could experience Dad's wild oscillations of personality may be doubted. Yet these phases do project outcomes that might await a mild old person under stress. The book may be hard to take for older readers in uncertain health, but otherwise opens up many real questions and potentials.

132 *Author:* Wilson, Angus
  Title: **Late Call.** London: Martin Secker & Warburg, 1964
  Genre: novel
  Commentary: Now that Sylvia Calvert, 64, has retired from manag-
  ing a seaside resort hotel in England, she can take a "late call" (sleep
  late) for a change. But her life will not be that easy after all. Sylvia
  and her husband move in with her widowed son, Harold, who lives
  in a new town in the Midlands. Sylvia isn't happy there, for several
  reasons: Harold is an overbearing, sometimes authoritarian father;
  Harold's three adult children are busy trying to find some individuality outside their father's control; and Sylvia's husband, Arthur, is a
  petty, conniving loafer who gambles away money he borrows from
  family and friends. Sylvia finds that although she wants to contribute to the family life, she can't find a role that will allow her to fit in.
      Readers gain an insight into Sylvia's character in the first chapter,
  which chronicles events that take place in the summer of 1911. Sylvia, a girl of ten, is compelled to become surrogate mother for her
  siblings because her mother is busy working all day. Her father, an
  alcoholic, abuses her severely. Consequently, Sylvia fears the risks
  of intimacy.
      Throughout the novel Sylvia attempts to "remake herself," to ad-
  just to her new surroundings. The turning point in her experience
  occurs when she is trapped in a sudden storm during a long walk;
  she rescues a young girl huddled under a tree and carries her away
  moments before the tree is struck by lightning. The girl's parents
  welcome Sylvia as a hero, and Sylvia and the girl develop a warm
  friendship. Sylvia finds herself being treated as an individual. The
  more she is with them, the more comfortable with herself she feels,
  and eventually she is able to exorcize the demons from her past and
  admit that although her childhood was unhappy, she can forgive her
  parents for not having been loving and affectionate toward her. Em-
  powered by these events, Sylvia is ready to help her family through
  several crises that arise suddenly. She resolves the pain of her past
  and faces the future with confidence.

133 *Author:* Woiwode, Larry
  Title: **Poppa John.** New York: Farrar, 1981
  Genre: novel
  Commentary: The predicament of many old people who find themselves deprived of an effective role is dramatized in this story of the
  actor Ned Daley, suddenly out of work. Now in his late sixties, Ned
  played the character Poppa John on a popular television soap opera

for twelve years. His character Poppa John was a wise, lovable, and helpful old man who was widely admired by other characters. Although Poppa John had a core of dedicated fans, network executives decided several months ago to cancel the program. So over the past few months, Poppa John became ill and "died" on the show. Ned has convinced himself that nothing he has done in his life, including his stint as the character Poppa John, has been worthwhile. He gets drunk regularly and is on the brink of a nervous breakdown. Eventually he learns that through his role as an actor many people's lives have been inspired and renewed. He begins to believe in himself again and to resolve the spiritual crisis in his life.

Ned's crisis has its roots in his feelings of loss, failure, and guilt surrounding the brutal murder of his father, a policeman who became involved with the mob. These events occurred when Ned was eleven years old. Since then Ned has never been able to forgive himself for not "saving" his father. Now it is two days before Christmas, and Ned is supposed to be shopping for a present for his wife, Celia.

Ned spends the day bar-hopping. Memories of his childhood resurface, and he is confronted again with feelings of guilt and remorse. Wherever he goes, he is plagued with entreaties from a variety of people who are devoted fans of his alter ego, Poppa John. Each of these people views Ned as a role model, mentor, or father figure. But Ned resists what he considers to be their neurotic attachments to Poppa John.

Near the end of the day, after a drunken flirtation with a salesperson, Ned passes out in a bar and is taken to the hospital by the police. There he is reunited with Celia. Although she is distraught over his self-destructive behavior, she stands by him and declares her love for him.

When Ned is sober again, Celia persuades him that his years spent acting the role of Poppa John have been worthwhile. She tells him that he made a difference for other people—even the ones who seemed to abuse what he provided. In fact, as she watched Ned prepare for "dying" as the character Poppa John, she was inspired to reevaluate her spiritual values. Her faith in Ned offers him hope for self-renewal. Ned feels confident that he can make this time of his life a transition from one role to another.

Stories

201 *Author:* Adler, Warren

Title: "The Angel of Mercy." In **The Sunset Gang.** New York: Viking, 1977

Genre: story

Commentary: Yetta Klugerman, whose "old age had shaped and gnarled her...completely," is the "village character" of Sunset Village, a retirement complex in Florida. Mrs. Klugerman is known sarcastically, and yet affectionately, as the "angel of mercy" because each day she insists on visiting several people who are convalescing at home. Although no one knows much about her personal background, Mrs. Klugerman has "become something of a legend." The story provides realistic glimpses of daily life in a retirement village, reveals how old people deal with the ever-present reality of death, and suggests on a metaphorical level that if an angel could take bodily form, perhaps it would most appropriately take the form of an ancient woman who dispenses candy and friendly advice with each of her visits.

When one of the residents of Sunset Village, Max Shinsky, returns home from the hospital to recuperate from his third heart attack, Mrs. Klugerman is there the first day for a visit. Each day she visits Max early in the morning, and after a time his physical condition improves. At that point she ceases her visits to Max.

Max is struck by this strange and mysterious woman. He begins to think, "She is more than what she says she is." Soon he becomes obsessed with the idea that this old woman is not a human being at all—but a ministering angel who has the power to heal people. As he gathers evidence, his obsession is fueled. One day he discovers that she has not returned to her condominium. He gains entry and finds no sign of human habitation. He lingers for a moment to commune with her spirit and is convinced that she really was an angel of mercy.

202 *Author:* Alvarez, Eduardo A.
   Title: "Calle Espana." In **Love Is Ageless: Stories about Alzheimer's
      Disease.** Ed. by Jessica Bryan. Oakland, Calif.: Serala Pr., 1987
   Genre: story
   Commentary: The narrator, a physician in his seventies, recalls two
   unsettling experiences from his youth, the first when he was a child
   of five, the second when a youth of fifteen. Both times he encoun-
   tered images of dementia that terrified him, overwhelmed him, and
   left emotional scars that have never healed. Through these experiences he gained a heightened awareness of the potential for despair
   and mystery in the human condition.
      He characterizes his Spanish town as "a sleepy, peaceful place"
   where "nothing happened but what had happened before." Extended families live in enclaves throughout the town. The Alvarez
   family, for example, lives on Calle Espana. As a boy of five, the narrator briefly enjoyed a special relationship with an old woman, the
   wife of his mother's cousin. She surrounded herself with many
   beautiful birds, and the boy saw her house as a place of magic. But
   soon the old woman began to manifest behavioral changes that
   frightened him. One day, as he waited in the courtyard, he saw her
   inside through an open door. She was naked, raving madly, her
   body fouled with feces, her hair disheveled. The narrator concludes,
   "What I saw, nothing in my life had prepared me for."
      Ten years later he has a similar encounter with the sister of this
   old woman, who also became reclusive and demented. He recalls
   feeling "suddenly very old" when he left Calle Espana street.
   Haunted by these encounters, and feeling that nothing there would
   surprise him anymore, the young man leaves his village to attend
   medical school at the university.

203 *Author:* Auchincloss, Louis
   Title: "Suttee." In **Second Chance: Tales of Two Generations.** New
      York: Houghton, 1970
   Genre: story
   Commentary: Agnes Lynn, a 67-year-old widow, starts a new life
   trying to adjust to changed circumstances, and she soon discovers
   that her life has been her husband's life, especially his business career. But now, without that connection to his company, she feels set
   adrift and isolated from meaningful contacts. Her story provides
   several insights into the psychological complexity of widowhood,
   the relationship between a husband's career and his wife's identity,
   the power of "duty" as a determinant for behavior, and the difficulty

of overcoming traditional roles and behaviors to take on new risks of involvement.

A 50-year-old senior partner of the firm proposes friendship and alliance; he views her as a way to maintain ties with the continuity of the past and the traditions that built the company. They begin by spending one day a week together, but soon they spend time with others from the company. Agnes discovers, to her dismay, that she and the younger man are viewed as a couple. Before long he proposes marriage, and she seems at the point of accepting his proposal. Eventually she decides that she cannot marry this younger man.

She capitulates, metaphorically, to the "suttee"; just as Hindu wives hurled themselves onto their husbands' funeral pyres, Agnes allows herself to be consumed by her warped sense of "duty" to the memory of her dead husband. At one point she believes, "The world would forgive love, at any age, in any old fool." Yet she retreats from what life has to offer, and in the last line of the story, she is shown realizing she now stands in line with all of the other widows who have gone before her to be consumed in the sacrificial fires.

204 *Author:* Bates, H. E.
   Title: "Where the Cloud Breaks" (1961). In **The Best of H. E. Bates.**
      Boston: Little, 1963
   Genre: story
   Commentary: The negative effects of self-imposed isolation in an aged person are illustrated in this story of Colonel Gracie, a retired officer in the British Army Signal Corps. To Colonel Gracie, all modern forms of communication are symbols of what is confusing, fearful, and unmanageable in his old age. Hence he has turned his back on television, radio, telephone and newspaper. Now suffering from episodes of dementia, Colonel Gracie finds himself ever more alienated and alone. His only human contact is with a neighbor, an indulgent spinster named Miss Wilkinson, with whom he communicates using semaphores. Instead of seeking help, Colonel Gracie hardens himself against his neighbor's willingness to embrace change.

   Colonel Gracie clearly is demented. He has taken to eating only eggs, he cannot remember what day it is, and he has forgotten a teatime engagement with Miss Wilkinson. When he arrives late for tea, she surprises him by showing him a gift from her sister—a used television set. She thinks he will be pleased by her determination to embrace this modern technology. But Colonel Gracie is enraged. He believes that she has broken a sacred trust between them. Miss Wilkinson says, "Yes, but there are other viewpoints. One comes to realise that." But Colonel Gracie will not yield. He is terrified at the prospect of being forced to adapt to a changing world. He expects her to return the set. Later she says, "Now we'll have to agree to differ." When he becomes abusive, she becomes obstinate. When he leaves, he tells her he will signal her if he wants something. She drops the next bombshell. She won't be answering any more signals.

Devastated by this turn of events, Colonel Gracie returns to his house. He thinks of sending her a message, "Please forgive me." But he cannot act.

205 *Author:* Bausch, Richard

Title: "Wise Men at Their end." In **Spirits and Other Stories.** New York: Simon & Schuster, 1987

Genre: story

Commentary: Theodore Weathers, 83, is a gruff, impatient man who isn't afraid to say what's on his mind. He doesn't appreciate sentimental gestures, and he resists being categorized as old and useless. He has been a widower for twenty years. When his daughter introduces him to an old woman who has also been widowed, he resists her unsubtle attempt at matchmaking. The interaction between these two old people is a refreshing example of the subtlety and unpredictability that can be found in relationships in old age.

Theodore's daughter-in-law, Judy, has decided to take him on as her special case after her husband dies. She thinks she knows exactly what he needs, and she doesn't hesitate to advise him about how to change in order to enjoy a fruitful old age. He deeply resents her intrusiveness, her patronizing attitude, her "proprietary irony." Before she comes to see him after work, he enjoys hours of peaceful living. He reads while lying in bed, sits on the porch and sips whiskey, and dozes quietly until she arrives.

One day Judy invites Alice Karnes, a volunteer at the hospital where Judy works, to visit Theodore. Like Theodore, she is a former math teacher and lover of fine things. While going down the stairs to fetch some whiskey for his guests, Theodore's knee gives way and he falls down the stairs. When he wakes up in the hospital, the first person he sees is Alice Karnes. Theodore is testy, mean-tempered, and even abusive to the old woman, but she holds her own against him.

A month later Theodore is released from the hospital. Now safe in his house, he acknowledges feeling real fear about dying. He begins to resolve some of these fears. While he sits on the porch in the afternoon, Alice stays with him while Judy is at work. Although lacking an easy resolution of the strained relationship between the two old people, the story ends with a sense of hope: "They sat there in the shade of the porch. They looked like a couple long married, still in the habit of love."

The title refers to a line in Dylan Thomas' "Do Not Go Gentle into That Good Night" ("Though wise men at their end know dark is right, / Because their words had forked no lightning. . . ."). Theodore Weathers is a man who rages at being categorized as old and helpless; he will never go "gentle" into his old age.

206   *Author:* Berriault, Gina
      Title: "The Diary of K. W." In **The Infinite Passion of Expectation: Twenty-Five Stories.** San Francisco: North Point Pr., 1982
      Genre: story
      Commentary: This is the strangely engaging soliloquy of an elderly loser who keeps a diary over several weeks as she starves physically and spiritually. K. W. has been fired as cafeteria substitute helper at a grammar school because she couldn't bear feeding the children to grow up in misery. From her rambling thoughts, one learns that K. W. had been a high school valedictorian; she had once been married; she has read philosophy; she has painted; she has worked most of her life on her feet. She fantasizes about loving a young man who has moved upstairs. The brief final entry is headed "The Last Day."

      What is the appeal of this ugly stick of an old woman who seems determined to despise herself, to wince at the joy of lovers, to starve to death? Well, she is thoughtful; she has a wry wit; she is compassionate. One likes her company. The core of K. W. seems to be her fearful, pessimistic, but tender and loving heart—perhaps the heart of many lonely old people who exist in impoverished solitude.

207   *Title:* "The Bystander"
      Commentary: This story provides a view of the aged human wreckage stored up in public institutions. A son goes to visit his aging father, whose violent breakdown has landed him in a psychiatric hospital. The son is vividly aware of the alienation and sensitivity of the patients. The small talk is ghastly. In a final epiphany, the son sees his father in other male patients: "He was the parent who breaks down under the eyes of his child, the parent in the last years when all the circumstances of his life have got him trussed and dying, while the child stands and watches the end of the struggle and then walks away to catch a streetcar."

208 *Title:* "Nocturne"
Commentary: Empathy for the difficulties of helpless aging is here shown with rare insight. Eulalia, a dependent old woman and would-be hanger-on of the Rand family, is seen through the eyes of a younger dependent, the young daughter-in-law, Val, whose husband has deserted her and her two children. Val sees in Eulalia the ugly senile waif she herself may become one day. Though instructed by her mother-in-law not to give Eulalia food, Val when left alone invites the old woman to supper.

Two other rewarding stories are "The Infinite Passion of Expectation" (the possibilities of new love for an old psychologist) and "Like a Motherless Child" (a quietly tragic picture of a lonely but spirited old woman).

209 *Author:* Bly, Carol
Title: "Gunnar's Sword" (1979). In **Backbone: Short Stories by Carol Bly.** Minneapolis, Minn.: Milkweed Editions, 1985
Genre: story
Commentary: Life continues to challenge and inspire Harriet White, an 82-year-old resident of the Lutheran Nursing Home in the small Minnesota town of Jacob. Harriet is alert, compassionate, hard working, an indispensable part of the nursing-home community. She comments sensibly on the relationships between old people in an institutionalized setting and on the subtle stereotyping and patronizing of old people. Her experiences in the story also illustrate the complex interactions between the generations, and the old person's never-ending search for meaning.

Actually Harriet is not part of the class of "old" people who live in the nursing home. Eight years ago she came to live here to be close to her husband, who needed skilled nursing care. A year ago he suffered a debilitating stroke, and now he lives in a vegetative state. Despite the trauma of her personal crisis, Harriet has become a role model for the other, less-fortunate old people in the home.

Bly's story recreates one crucial day in Harriet's life. After a busy morning visiting some of the residents and organizing a birthday party for another resident, she is visited by her son. He tells her that he has sold the family farm. Stunned by this turn of events, Harriet makes her daily visit to her husband to vent her feelings of anger and betrayal. Although he cannot respond to her words, she feels comforted by talking to him. Then she goes for a long walk and makes her way to the family farm. There she experiences a mysterious presence—perhaps a symbolic representation of her mortality.

Her response to this vision restores her energy and spirit. She reconciles herself to her fate and returns to the nursing home.

210 *Author:* Brooks, Gwendolyn
Title: "Death of Grandmother" (1953). In **The World of Gwendolyn Brooks**. New York: Harper, 1971
Genre: story
Commentary: The repulsive dying of an old woman is witnessed by daughter and granddaughter. This terse narrative brings out the awesomeness of death even in the humblest of victims.

The account comes through the consciousness of young Maud Martha, the protagonist of the collection of biographical sketches, *Maud Martha*. Grandmother is seen as a "semi-corpse": ugly, repellent, capable only of responding to questions with "Hawh." The isolation of death is realized in "this ordinary woman who had suddenly become a queen, for whom presently the most interesting door of them all would open, who, lying locked in boards with her 'hawhs,' yet towered, triumphed over them, while they stood there asking the stupid questions people ask the sick. . . ."

The callous irritability of an overworked hospital staff is voiced by the nurse who bitterly refuses to fetch a bedpan for another patient.

Whan Maud returns home, her father has just been telephoned that the grandmother is dead—an announcement that brings back to Maud the loving, doting Gramma of her childhood.

211 *Author:* Cather, Willa
Title: "Neighbor Rosicky" (1928). In **Obscure Destinies**. New York: Knopf, 1932
Genre: story
Commentary: Here is a story of the beautiful aging of a Czech-Bohemian immigrant farmer. Anton Rosicky, originally a tailor, had worked in London and then New York, until he sickened of city life and moved west with his wife Mary, whom he had met on shipboard. As farmers, they have been industrious but never anxious. "They had been at one accord not to hurry through life, not to be always skimping and saving." They enjoy each other and their five generous sons. They are hospitable and good neighbors.

The action begins with Anton's doctor warning him of a bad heart. He is to take it easy and he tries to do so. A main concern is his beloved daughter-in-law, Polly, the American wife of his son Rudolph, a woman who finds farm life hard. He wins her affection by kindness; then, in a fatal act of paternal love, he overtaxes his heart by ploughing up thistles at her farm. As the doctor reflects at the graveyard, "Rosicky's life seemed to him complete and beautiful."

The story is long and possibly dated in its focus on the European immigrant. But it is artfully simple and eloquent of the beautiful aging of a man who has lived well despite hardship. Anton's own reminiscences not only help the present action but also show the values of the life review.

212   *Title:* "Old Mrs. Harris" (1931)
Genre: story (novella)
Commentary: A failing grandmother, Mrs. Harris, works behind the scenes to arrange a loan for granddaughter Vickie to attend college—a good deed symbolic of her quiet role as family guardian and spiritual supporter.

The time is probably early 1900s. The Templeton family have settled in an eastern Colorado town in an ineffectual migration from their feudal culture in Tennessee to this bustling Western democracy where they do not thrive despite originally high hopes. The mother, Victoria, has been brought up as a spoiled darling; she is not popular with her new neighbors. The father, Hillary, has fine manners but does not get on; he has tied up the family funds in investment. Young Vickie, a special favorite of her grandmother, is bright. Under encouragement from her bookish neighbor, Mrs. Rosen, she studies for a university scholarship. She wins it, only to find that she must still raise $300 for expenses—a sum her father cannot manage. With humble courage, the dignified Mrs. Harris ventures to ask help from Mrs. Rosen, who undertakes to have her husband, the town storekeeper, advance the loan. Mrs. Harris, already failing, quietly dies, thankful for her life and family.

This is a wonderful portrait of the supportive grandmother and of her intergenerational effectiveness. The story ends with an eloquent appeal for the young to notice such qualities.

213   *Author:* Cheever, John
Title: "The World of Apples" (1966). In **The Stories of John Cheever.** New York: Knopf, 1973
Genre: story
Commentary: Asa Bascomb is a famous American poet who has retired to a remote Italian villa and begun to question his reason for being. Although he has been awarded numerous awards for his poetry, foremost in his mind is the question, "Why haven't I won the

Nobel Prize?" The title of his most popular book of poems is *The World of Apples,* a work that draws on his New England roots and inspires its readers with images of lightness and purity. But an unexpected sight on a routine afternoon drive overturns Bascomb's peaceful retirement and initiates a period of intense self-scrutiny. At age 82, Asa Bascomb confronts his deepest fears and resolves the contradictions between anxiety and love that have dominated his life. After the prolonged agony of this self-examination, which nearly leaves him incapacitated, Bascomb regains a measure of self-respct and creativity.

What happens to trigger this self-examination? One day while touring the countryside, he encounters by chance a couple copulating in the woods. He is overwhelmed by this encounter, and immediately his moral sensibility is overturned. Everything becomes unclean. He begins to write in earnest, but everything he pens is scatalogical humor, obscene limericks, pornographic prose. After a day's work he burns his writings in the stove, but he cannot purge himself of his polluted soul. All of his experiences reinforce his conviction that he is depraved. After two weeks of this torment, he is paralyzed by despair.

The source of his excessive self-flagellation is his growing sense of anxiety. For despite his successes, Asa Bascomb is anxious and unsure of his past accomplishments, and he has lost a sense of direction for his present situation. He can't understand why his admirers have fixed upon *The World of Apples* as his greatest accomplishment, and he suffers from anxiety over the possible loss of his memory in old age.

As a desperate measure to find solace, Bascomb makes a whimsical pilgrimage to a local shrine to exorcise the demon from his soul. He gains some relief from the experience, but the next day he experiences a more significant pilgrimage when he is put in touch with a significant childhood memory that helps him recover the gifts of innocence and love that were the legacy of his childhood.

214 *Author:* Coon, Betty
Title: "Daisies." In **Women and Aging: An Anthology by Women.**
Ed. by Jo Alexander and others. Corvallis, Ore.: Calyx, 1986
Genre: story
Commentary: The obstinacy of an old Italian widow in resisting manipulation by her children marks this brief story of Maria Pavese. Nearly blind, with shrinking interests, Maria wants to be free of her old house in its run-down neighborhood. But she stiffens under the

importunate urging to move out that comes from her daughter Gina, her flashy son-in-law Max, the hungry real estate lady, and Father Lombardi.

Actually the house tires Maria, as does the memory of her husband, Ernesto, who "worked on this place the way some people climb a mountain," constantly repainting, redecorating, raising a plethora of tomatoes. One thing she does care for: the daisies that bloom in the backyard. Knowing that she may give up the house, she will not do it under pressure. After she has insulted son-in-law, realtor, and priest into leaving her parlor, Maria sits on her back porch, dreaming of all the gladiolas, tulips, narcissus, and mums she is going to plant.

215 *Author:* Dokey, Richard
Title: "The Autumn of Henry Simpson" (1978). In **August Heat: Stories by Richard Dokey.** Chicago: Story Pr., 1982
Genre: story
Commentary: The aching loneliness of a widowed old age is deeply felt by Henry Simpson, whose life "was like a museum, where he wandered from room to room trying to guess what the people had been like." His empty days are marked by melancholy and guilt, as he wonders how his life could have been better and what it all could have meant. A seismic disruption occurs when his over-solicitous daughter tricks him into visiting the old people's home she plans for him to enter. Seldom has such a home been seen in more repellent light than the Mid-Valley Retirement Home as it strikes upon the horrified consciousness of Henry. He runs from the home in panic. Sitting alone later in the park, he comes at last to a kind of peace over his own mortality.

This powerful story embodies several themes of aging: the older person's loss of independence; the problems of adult children in looking after aging parents; the quality of retirement homes; the ordeal of spousal bereavement; life review in old age; and the spiritual challenge of diminishing vitality.

216 *Title:* "The Teacher" (1977)
Commentary: An integenerational appeal lifts Mr. Sexton, an old English teacher, out of the arid tedium of his days. Sexton is fat, unprepossessing, often laughed at by his students. One day a young lad, George, seeks him out for advice on his sweetheart's pregnancy. George is afraid of the parents. He feels he must marry the girl. He is not ready. Sexton tries desperately to skirt the boy's dilemma

while still returning the boy's friendliness. At last he is stirred by a review of his own unhappy marriages, by a recognition of his own retreat from life, and by a vision of his real identification with the boy. He then makes an offer—what the boy has evidently wanted to hear—to pay for an abortion. He believes it to be better than loveless wedlock.

217 *Author:* Fisher, M. F. K.
Title: "Another Love Story." In **Sister Age.** New York: Knopf, 1983
Genre: story
Commentary: Sister Age is devoted to stories of aging persons, as framed by the Foreword. In Zurich in 1936, the narrator had found in a rummage shop an old portrait of Ursula von Ott, a strange woman standing patiently before images of her departed son. The narrator thought of her as Sister Age (after St. Francis, who spoke of Brother Pain) and carried the portrait with her as a touchstone as she continued her curiosity about aging. Some of the stories are less accessible because of European settings or high fantasy. Toward the end of the volume, "Notes on a Necessary Pact" contains several excellent observations and fictive fragments on aging.

"Another Love Story" is a touching account of late love somehow blighted by cultural differences. Marnie Allen, divorced, brings two young daughters to Morro Bay on the California coast. Here they meet a widower, Mr. Henshaw, a "handsome, brown old fellow" who hires out his boat. He befriends the girls and takes them all on trips. The children urge their mother to marry him. He later proposes gently and eloquently. The match seems plausible, especially since uranium investment has made him rich and he could take care of all of them. He takes them on a final trip to rough water despite her unwillingness. Coming in: "That was to show you how brave you really can be." But she does not respond, and the family leaves him forever.

218 *Title:* "Answer in the Affirmative" (1982)
Commentary: As a young wife, the narrator, while staying at her mother's, is caressed by old Mr. Ardamanian, traveling mender and cleaner of rugs. The sexuality of his contact is not denied: the two might well have gone to the couch if the husband had not returned. What keeps this episode from being "dirty"? A partial answer may be that the young wife has been faithful to her husband in all other ways; she feels no lust or guilt over this strange encounter with a gentle old man. Somehow it blesses her in her womanhood.

219 *Title:* "The Reunion"
Commentary: Professor Lucien Revenant, who has aged while dawdling over his unfinished doctoral thesis, plans a little party for "five
dear people he had neglected as they all grew older and more preoccupied by their own dwindling parties." It turns out that all are
dead, the Professor having had his funeral that morning. This tale is
a startling reminder to seize the day. (The word "revenant" means
one who returns after death.)

220 *Author:* Forster, E. M.
Title: "The Road from Colonus" (1911). In **The Collected Tales of
E. M. Forster.** New York: Knopf, 1947
Genre: story
Commentary: This powerful fantasy suggests the personal expansion that can await the questing spirit in old age. Mr. Lucas, dread-
ing a trivial old age, has a mystic experience while on a tour of
Greece, a country he had always wanted to explore. Wandering
along a road, he sees a spring of water issuing from the hollow
trunk of a massive old tree. He enters the tree and rests in its surrounding comfort. Suddenly an awareness invades him, a sense of
beauty in all things, intelligible and good. But his touring party
overtakes him. They overcome his passionate desire to stop at the
inn near this miraculous tree. They bear him back to England,
where he is last seen fussing and complaining over small inconve-
niences, victim of the trivial old age he had feared.

In summary, Mr. Lucas had come to the very brink of a new per-
sonhood only to have everyday considerations tragically pull him
back. The title refers to the sacred grove at Colonus, near Athens.
There Oedipus, the tragic king of Thebes, came to die and meet his
gods; and from there Mr. Lucas, so to speak, took the sad road back.

Another fantasy tale, somewhat involved, is "The Point of It"
(1928). Here the main character is carried from youth through old
age to the after-life, where he learns the true point of the life he had
only skirted.

221 *Author:* Frame, Janet
Title: "The Bath." In **You Are Now Entering the Human Heart.**
London: Women's Pr., 1983
Genre: story
Commentary: An old New Zealand widow takes a bath and visits
her husband's grave—that is the sum of this moving brief story.

What gives it exceptional force is its documentation of the physical and mental suffering imposed on the very old by a simple chore like taking a bath.

As the story opens on a cold spring day, Mrs. Harraway (always referred to as simply "she") buys cut flowers for her anniversary visit to the grave of her husband, dead seventeen years. Then she prepares for the bath that these days she physically can't manage more than weekly or fortnightly. Carefully she arranges the towel, the nightclothes to change into, the chair to aid in her escape from the tub. She descends into the tub much as one might descend a cliff. After prolonging the comfort of the water and delaying the ordeal of leaving it, she tries without luck to emerge. Only after a fearful struggle does she finally manage.

Her visit to the cemetery the next day is marked by a rare mildness in the wind. Among the graves of husband and parents, she finds something like peace, a serenity that renders her daily life all the more awful by contrast. She returns cheerlessly to her "world narrowing and growing darker," a world bristling with the tiny awesome obstacles that hinder and close down even the little routines. The image of the waiting bath is what fills her consciousness at the close.

"The treachery of the body" has rarely been so sensitively recorded. This woman's heroic struggles raise such questions as how long an elderly person can remain independent. Those struggles also command admiration.

222   *Author:* Freeman, Mary E. Wilkins
      Title: "A Mistaken Charity" (1887). In **Selected Stories of Mary E.
           Wilkins Freeman.** Ed. by Marjorie Pryse. New York: Norton,
           1983
      Genre: story
      Commentary: Two aged sisters rebel against the "mistaken charity" of those who would deprive them of independence for their own good. The setting is New England in the last century; the central issue—of institutionalizing the elderly—is contemporary.

      Harriet Shattuck, who is stubborn and proud, and her sister, Charlotte, who is blind and a bit simple, eke out a living in a ruined cottage, raising and harvesting a few crops, and taking gifts from neighbors. They are plain unambitious folk, the last of the Shattuck family long settled there. A vigorously philanthropic townswoman, Mrs. Simonds, benignly conspires with a well-to-do widow and the minister to install the sisters in an Old Ladies' Home, which turns out to be unendurably proper and stuffy. The sisters run away and return to their home, proud and happy though the means of their survival will steadily diminish.

An eloquent symbol is the "chinks" of lights that the blind Charlotte sees at moments of happiness and that fill her vision on the final homecoming.

223   *Author:* Hall, Donald
       Title: "The Ideal Bakery." In **The Ideal Bakery: Stories by Donald Hall.** San Francisco: North Point Pr., 1987
       Genre: story
       Commentary: The narrator of the story, a man nearing 60, recalls the special times during the spring of 1939 when his father took him for breakfast to the Ideal Bakery "just over the New Haven line from Hamden." His recollection of these idyllic Saturday mornings gives way to a listing of the devastating losses experienced by the boy's family and friends in the intervening fifty years. Those Saturday mornings were the last perfect days of his childhood. When they were lost, something of the innocence and purity of childhood was lost as well. The story suggests that early memories can leap across a lifetime of suffering and loss to lend their grace to the aging person.

After recreating the perfect charm of these mornings, the narrator recites a shocking litany of death and decline in the intervening years: his father's alcoholism and death in middle age, his mother's struggle with mental illness during World War II, his sister's breast cancer, and his mother's disabling arthritis and her recent placement in a nursing home. He also notes that Gus, the owner of the Ideal Bakery, was afflicted with Alzheimer's disease. How can anyone face such an accumulation of misfortune? He can find no explanation for why some people lead quiet, uneventful lives while others experience recurring tragedies. He can only cite one compensation: "Several times a week I am ten years old sitting in a booth at the Ideal Bakery, loving my tender father who smiles across the tabletop."

224   *Title:* "The First Woman"
       Commentary: This story illustrates the folly of trying to age as the perpetual young lover. When William Boulter was 16, he had intercourse with a 24-year-old married woman on the last day of World War II. Since then he married several times and went from lover to

lover. Now 51 and teaching in Seattle, Boulter learns by chance that the woman also lives in the area.

Half hoping to recapture his adolescent experience, Boulter visits her. But his insensitive remarks, excessive drinking, and tactless attempts at seduction infuriate her. She throws him out after he insinuates that she is having a love affair with an artist whose works hang in her living room. She calls him "an old fool who takes young women to bed with you." He leaves, but he gives no indication of changing.

Another story in the collection, "Widowers' Woods," depicts the last day of two New England widowers who have developed distinct routines after being widowed for two years. Their separate experiences are united through the metaphor of the "widowers' woods," which stands for a mysterious and fanciful place into which these old men disappear when they die. Their experiences reflect the fate of widowers who cease to have a practical function in the world.

225 *Author:* Hansen, Ron
    Title: "Red-Letter Days." In **Nebraska: Stories.** New York: Atlantic
       Monthly Pr., 1989
    Genre: story
    Commentary: This story consists of twenty-one entries from an old man's diary over four months (January–May). The entries portray a character who is active and engaged with life in his old age. Cecil, nearly 70, is a former lawyer who lives in a small town in Nebraska. His diary reveals his affection and love for his wife, Emma, his engagement in church and community affairs, his love of reading about history and politics, and his continual interactions with a network of friends. He maintains an active, healthy outlook on life, despite increasingly suffering from numerous aches and pains, and he spends time with old friends who are experiencing more serious physical decline (e.g., cancer, Alzheimer's).

Cecil is devoted to golf. He has been playing the game for sixty years, and he still shoots in the seventies. He is a student of the game, has many fixed opinions about the history of the game and the best golfers, and plays regularly with several friends from town. He recalls his best days of golfing as "red-letter days." His philosophy of life is summed up in the statement, "Even a really bad day of golf is better than a good day of work." He lavishes his love and attention on one young golfer he calls Wild Bill. He treats the young man like his grandson, although the two are not related. Cecil is sure that this young man, who is a year away from college, has the potential of becoming a professional golfer. Cecil teaches the young man all that he knows about the game, and he encourages William to attend a university where he can refine his skills.

Cecil's character is revealed through the accumulation of entries. References to his attending AA meetings, losing his driver's license, and leaving the legal profession suggest some of the obstacles he has had to overcome. But those shortcomings always remain in the background. No climactic event dominates the entries. Cecil and his wife celebrate her sixty-seventh birthday and they attend the funeral of a good friend. Most of Cecil's days are spent puttering around the house, visiting friends in town, and playing golf.

226 *Author:* Higgins, Joanna
   Title: "The Courtship of Widow Sobcek." In **The Best American Short Stories, 1982.** Ed. by John Gardner and Shannon Ravenal. Boston: Houghton, 1982
   Genre: story
   Commentary: Love does not easily penetrate the Polish working-class culture of old John Jielewicz. John is too proud to accept care from his adult daughter, too independent and hot-tempered to accept the instruction of a non-Polish priest to consider God's love and the goodness of life. Like the staunch peasant he was in the Old Country, he lives in a world of chores and hardships, with only a fading memory of his long-dead wife.

   When John carries his lace curtains to the Widow Sobcek for washing, he has a sudden vision of her through the lace she holds up, a vision of someone younger, a girl like his lost Masha. Although he does not recognize this little miracle as a sign of the divine grace that the priest had told him to look for, over the next year John gravitates unconsciously to the homely hospitality of the widow. His daughter, like many adult children alarmed at new attachments in a single parent, sees this interest as unseemly, even a threat to her natural expectation of inheritance.

   John's fall on the ice, his hospitalization, and the sudden cessation of the widow's visits bring about his full awareness of love and commitment to it.

227 *Author:* Johnson, Josephine
   Title: "Old Harry." In **Winter Orchard and Other Stories.** New York: Simon & Schuster, 1935
   Genre: story
   Commentary: Two lonely old men find companionship and solace from a world that has turned its back on them. Their relationship

ends abruptly when one of the men, in despair because of failing health and the pressure of family obligations, ends his own life. Their story unflinchingly portrays the complex feelings experienced by old men in a society that seems to isolate, abandon, and even discard the old.

For ten years Pagsbrey, a retired professor, has spent his days in a museum where Old Harry is a guard. Over the years they have become friends, and each day they lunch together. Old Harry, who lives with a daughter and her large family, is a source of companionship for Pagsbrey and his link to the real world. He listens enthusiastically to Pagsbrey's rambling discourses and shares the details of his own household life.

Old Harry's greatest fear is that he will lose this job. His salary from the museum position is the primary source of income for the family. His feet are beginning to fail, and his fear of disability is the source of his greatest terror. One day Pagsbrey arrives and learns that Old Harry, who has arrived earlier that day, has been found lying dead outside the museum. He died after taking a bottle of poison. Pagsbrey is devastated, alone in the world. His days spent in the museum now are empty and unfulfilling. He seeks solace by imagining that Old Harry's struggle to survive represents something "permanent and beautiful," a timeless symbol of human suffering.

"The Preacher's Pilgrimage" tells the story of a black minister whose dream of making a journey to the Holy Land appears to be realized when his family and congregation agree that he should use the money from his "funeral" savings to finance the trip. He looks forward to this momentous journey because in his old age he has begun to doubt his spiritual gifts. But when he arrives in New York, he is refused passage on the ship because the trip is intended for white ministers only. Although his money is returned, he is left wandering aimlessly, afraid to face his people again.

228 *Author:* Knight, Wallace E.
   Title: "The Resurrection Man." In **The Atlantic Monthly,** 233:78–
      82 (April 1974)
   Genre: story
   Commentary: Alva Mason, a widower, lives in retirement in southern Indiana. When he discovers what he presumes to be a cancerous growth on his face, he begins to premeditate an end to his life. He spends more than a year planning an extraordinary suicide: Alva digs a hole in the side of a hill, fashions a lean-to covered with dirt

over the entrance, and with dynamite and hardware builds an "exploder." His plan: one day he will slip into the hole, the exploder will detonate, he will be buried alive, and no one will ever find his body. But when Alva tries to carry out his suicide, he is saved by the persistence of his will to live. Alva has experienced loneliness, fear, alienation, and despair in his old age. Yet when he finds himself scrunched into his death chamber and wanting only to survive, he realizes that his death will take care of itself. He wants to concentrate on living his life.

Alva once said, "Man needs something ungiving behind him to back him up." After his wife died, he moved twenty miles from town and lived at the foot of Ten Pole Mountain. During his retirement years he had that "ungiving" supportive force behind him. When he climbs out of his hole, he looks up at that mountain and muses, "I don't think I could have had a better place to live...if I had searched all over the world. This place is going to be here forever." This perspective on immortality suggests that now Alva is ready to live.

Knight's story is written in a folksy, matter-of-fact style, and the author characterizes Alva as a self-reliant man of the earth. In some respects Alva is never more alive than during the time he plans his own death. His ingenuity and self-control are remarkable.

229 *Author:* Labozzetta, Marisa
Title: "Making the Wine." In **When I Am an Old Woman I Shall Wear Purple: An Anthology of Short Stories and Poetry.** Ed. by Sandra Martz. Manhattan Beach, Calif.: Papier-Maché Pr., 1987

Genre: story
Commentary: We usually experience dementia as spectators of our stricken loved ones. In this story the dementia is vividly realized from the inside, through the cross-grained consciousness of an Italian woman as she tries to think of her husband Angelo, to whom she has been married for over fifty years.

She—or "Boss" as Angelo has always called her—recalls their early days near Rome, the country place they earned in America, the gardening, the Italian dishes, the wine-making, the raising of children. Angelo is always near, coming in from the garden, lunching, drinking coffee, listening to radio news, and—to her distaste—having nightly "love affairs" with her.

It gradually becomes apparent that Boss is living all this disconnectedly in the past. She has had a disabling attack while making wine. She now spills food at the table, she ruins the electric coffee pot by heating it over gas, she fails to recognize her son-in-law, she is incontinent. One senses the dismay of her daughter, especially when the mother is denied admission to a nursing home. With some shock, one realizes that Angelo is long dead, a discovery all the more poignant as the monologue ends with Boss asking Angelo to have a "love affair" tonight.

230 *Author:* MacDonald, D. R.
     Title: "Poplars." In **Eyestone: Stories by D. R. MacDonald.** Wainscott, N.Y.: Pushcart Pr., 1988
     Genre: story
     Commentary: A compelling intergenerational relationship is profiled in this story about an old Nova Scotia farmer who returns home after suffering a stroke. Thanks to his adult nephew's affection, determination, and caregiving skills, the old man can renew his life. The nephew recovers some childhood memories and gains insight into the will and courage of his uncle.

     Four months after Lauchie Chisholm has suffered a serious stroke, his nephew Neil arrives from California to help him recover. After many visits to the nursing home, Neil drives him back to the farm one morning. When they enter the house, they discover that it has been vandalized.

     Though disheartened, Lauchie isn't defeated. Near the road is a line of poplars that Lauchie planted years ago. As a child, Neil and other children used to race against Lauchie in the meadow above the poplars. When Neil now leaves his uncle unattended for a moment at the top of the hill, the old man starts his wheelchair down the slope toward the poplars and crashes into them. Neil races after him, and when he reaches the overturned wheelchair, he finds his uncle lying unhurt on the ground. The old man looks toward the trees and says, "I'm tougher than them. My heart and my head, too." Now that Lauchie has had his "run," he is ready to return to the farm house and resume his life.

231 *Title:* "Work"
     Commentary: The final separation of two old fellow laborers reveals the deep feeling and intense loyalty that can develop in male friendships. It also shows the fear with which old people often face institutionalization. Jack MacBain, disabled and presenile, is to move away into a senior citizen's home with his wife, Dal. His old

buddy, Norman, cannot see how life has changed and keeps butting in on the couple until the exasperated and over-burdened wife tells him to leave Jack alone. Saddened, Norman obeys.

232 *Title:* "Of One Kind"
Commentary: This story tells of the passion of a 70-year-old handyman for the blind old widow he works for. Red Donald, the handyman, is a friendly and trustworthy soul whose long attraction to Mrs. MacKay crystallizes into an open declaration, which she rejects, being content with her solitary life. They come from different worlds and different values. Just being old and alone is not enough to make them "of one kind."

233 *Author:* Malamud, Bernard
Title: "The Mourners" (1958). In **The Stories of Bernard Malamud.**
    New York: Farrar, 1983
Genre: story
Commentary: An old man who has lived a bad life is the center of this story laid in the slums of New York's East Side. Kessler, a retired egg inspector living on Social Security, long ago deserted his wife and children. A nasty, irascible character, he has lived alone for ten years in an untidy flat on the fifth floor, shunned by the other tenants as a dirty old man.

One day Kessler quarrels so bitterly with the janitor that the landlord, Gruber, orders him to vacate. Kessler refuses. A court eviction order is served. Kessler does not respond. The city marshal with two assistants bodily hauls Kessler, together with his junky furniture, down to the street on a snowy day. Other tenants carry Kessler and his belongings back upstairs. That night Gruber visits Kessler to appeal and threaten. When he returns the next morning to offer help in getting Kessler into a public home, Kessler has not moved. He sits on the floor mourning his rotten wasted life. Gruber, suffering from his own mistreatment of the old man, joins him on the floor as a fellow mourner.

234 *Title:* "In Retirement" (1973)
Commentary: The stirrings of erotic desire agitate a lonely old doctor. Simon Morris, 68, a widower with few friends, leads a depressive routine of studying Greek and walking around lower New York. One morning after a boldly attractive young woman passes

him in the apartment lobby, he discovers a letter she had dropped, lying on the floor. He cannot keep himself from reading it—a father's exhortation that this woman, Evelyn, abandon her loose sex life. Morris fantasizes about making love with Evelyn. He thinks how little an age difference should count between a young woman and an elderly but still virile man.

Quietly Simon learns more about Evelyn and eventually writes a letter inviting her, in a most dignified way, to make his acquaintance. As he sits in the lobby at mail time, Evelyn emerges from the elevator together with a lover. She opens the doctor's letter, shares it with her lover, then tears it into shreds and flings them in the doctor's direction. "The fragments come at him like a blast of wind-driven snow."

235 *Author:* Mann, Thomas
   Title: "Death in Venice" (1911). In **Death in Venice and Other Stories**. Trans. by Kenneth Burke. New York: Knopf, 1965
   Genre: story
   Commentary: What can happen in the old age of a disciplined person who has always suppressed the passionate needs of life? In this long, troubling story, an aging novelist yields to the sensual drives that he has ignored over a lifetime of creative discipline.

Gustave Aschenbach, celebrated as the artistic voice of his age, is so focused on his writing that he even hesitates to travel, for fear of not completing his career. Nonetheless a strange intuition prompts him to leave Munich for a needed rest in summer climes. So he comes to Venice, the great resort city of the European south.

Here he notices a lovely Polish lad, divine in beauty, a living symbol of Eros, god of love. Aschenbach slips into an infatuation quite in subversion of his serious disposition. Though never a word is exchanged, Aschenbach sinks deeper into his obsession. He follows the boy through the streets. He beautifies his own aging head. All the while the city of Venice sinks into a plague of cholera that it conceals from its visitors. Aschenbach learns the danger, but is too infatuated to warn the youth's family. At the end, on the youth's final day on the beach, Aschenbach succumbs to the plague as he watches the lad apparently beckoning to him from across the water.

Mann is acclaimed as a philosophical novelist able to weave intellectual issues into a narrative fabric. The attention of a serious reader will be rewarded by his command of atmosphere, his richness of description, his suggestive use of symbol, his thoughtful asides.

236 *Author:* Matthews, Jack

Title: "First the Legs and Last the Heart" (1973). In **Dubious Persuasions: Short Stories by Jack Matthews.** Baltimore: Johns Hopkins Univ. Pr., 1981

Genre: story

Commentary: Any adult son or daughter who has gone looking for a confused parent who has wandered off among strangers will understand the dismay of this narrator on finding his old Dad in a wrecked telephone booth, keeping a senseless watch over rush-hour traffic and quite unready to budge. The leap of empathy by which the son resolves his father's deadlocked confusion might not appear as a prescription in a gerontology manual, but the story does enlarge the possibilities of caring.

The son tries a battery of approaches, from pointing out rationally that the booth is a useless place to stay, to urging emotionally that he himself has got to get home. Dad remains perfectly satisfied where he is. In the comedy that follows, the son improvises mad conversation with a dour woman in a nearby laundromat as he watches Dad. He reads the dreary schlock of an old romance magazine. At last, impelled to support his father against an unfeeling public, he returns to the booth and with staunch sympathy urges his father: "Hang on, Dad! Stay in there, old Buddy!"

At hearing so much expected of him, Dad replies that he really isn't as young as he used to be; would his son take over now? The son relieves Dad of this absurd duty, telling Dad to rest and wait at the laundromat. In the closing lines, he watches Dad: "His moves were those of a man coming home from work—tired, but satisfied, kind of, and full of a realization of something accomplished and fulfilled, too deep for expression, and, yes, too deep for words."

237 *Title:* "The Eternal Mortgage" (1979)

Commentary: The pressure in old age to come to terms with one's failures is illustrated in this story of an old man's remorse. The narrator, a dealer in second-hand books, tells how this strange old man, looking "a little wrong," came to his trailer searching for copies of *Lucy Lets Her Hair Down,* a pornographic photo-book published in the 1930s. The old man buys it and asks to be told of any other copies that turn up. Bit by bit, he reveals that he had posed for this sordid publication for twenty-five dollars. He has lived in agony for having sinned, in fear of the divine judgment that awaits him. His one hope is that "if I can only live long enough, I may buy the last one that exists."

Years later, the book-dealer comes upon another copy. He calls the person named as contact, only to find that the old man had been found dead in his rented room. Overcome by the "tired and hopeless evil" shown in the pictures, the narrator takes the book to his incinerator and burns it.

238 *Author:* Minot, Stephen
Title: "The Tide and Isaac Bates" (1973). In **Crossings: Stories by Stephen Minot.** Champaign: Univ. of Illinois Pr., 1975
Commentary: An old man, unable to respond adequately to complex feelings of personal loss and grief, experiences a gradual unraveling of his self-control, his faith in himself, and the basis of his relationship with his daughter.

Isaac Bates is a self-made millionaire who is used to controlling his environment and getting exactly what he wants out of life. But now his wife lies dying of cancer in a local hospital, and Isaac has just carelessly wrecked his boat in a fierce New England storm. He and his 18-year-old daughter, Cory, barely survive the wreck. When Isaac and his daughter return to the house, his grief begins to play tricks on him. He transfers his feelings of loneliness and separation to his daughter. He views her as a woman for the first time. The atmosphere of the darkened house becomes charged with a sexual tension.

Cory is grieving too, but the two characters are not able to communicate the subtlety of their thoughts and feelings to each other. Isaac is alone with his memories. Confused and overwrought with emotions he cannot control, Isaac attacks his daughter with a fierce sexual energy. She fends him off, but the basis of their relationship lies in ruins. They interact "like figures in a waiting room, afraid to touch each other even with words."

239 *Title:* "Small Point Bridge" (1969).
Genre: story
Commentary: Isaac Bates, an arrogant, self-assured man in his seventies learns that he does not have dominion over the natural world, that time is running out for him in old age, and that a meaningful human relationship—even at this stage of life—can serve as an adequate buffer against the tides that control his life.

Isaac Bates made his fortune by building a cannery and selling fishcakes. Widowed for two years, he lives alone across the bay from his cannery. Isaac's neighbor, Seth, maintenance man at the cannery for the past nineteen years, has lived all that time on Small Point, a "useless nob of land" owned by Isaac. Isaac visits Seth to take care of the "small point" of collecting rent. Both men know that if Seth stays on the land for another day without paying rent, he will, according to law, become the owner of the land and the house.

Neither yields to the other. As the two men struggle on the bridge outside of Seth's house, an ice jam undercuts the pilings of the cannery, and the entire facility drops into the bay. The two men retreat to Seth's house. Now the conflict over squatter's rights seems unimportant. What matters is that both old men face this loss, as well as their remaining years, together. The two men commune for the first time as equals and begin to find a bulwark against their human frailty.

240 *Author:* Mungoshi, Charles

Title: "Who Will Stop the Dark?" (1980). In **The Setting Sun and the Rolling World: Selected Stories by Charles Mungoshi.** London: Heinemann, 1987

Genre: story

Commentary: The power of grandparenting is shown in this African story. Sekuru, an old man, acts as a surrogate father, teacher, and companion to his 13-year-old grandson, Zakeo, whose father has been paralyzed in an accident. Through the old man's gentle and patient efforts, the boy begins to prepare for the new responsibilities that he will face in his family life.

In the Zimbabwean culture the father is the head of the household. Now Zakeo's father spends his days weaving baskets—a woman's occupation. Neither he nor his wife speak to the boy about this crisis in their family. Zakeo is left to figure things out for himself. He even begins to believe rumors that his mother is a witch and that she has cast a spell upon her husband in order to usurp his authority.

Zakeo's mother resents having been thrust into a new role as head of the household. She receives no support from her community. She also harbors a deep-seated anger toward the old man because she thinks he is undermining her authority and corrupting her son. She orders Zakeo to stay away from his grandfather and to attend school every day.

Troubled by these fears, the boy spends every possible moment with Sekuru. Their intergenerational relationship is central to the story. Sekuru loves his grandson, and he is careful not to undermine the authority of the boy's parents. He listens attentively to the boy's dreams and patiently teaches him what he knows about the individual's relationship to the natural world. But he realizes that what he can provide for the boy is limited. At the end of the story, Sekuru acknowledges that the boy's transition to manhood depends on his staying in school and adapting to the new dynamics within his household.

241 *Author:* Munro, Alice
Title: "Mrs. Cross and Mrs. Kidd." In **The Moons of Jupiter.** New York: Macmillan, 1982
Genre: story
Commentary: Hilltop Home is a gallery of decrepit people—the middle-aged Mongoloid, the woman searching for nonexistent vital papers, the woman with the terrible goiter, the urine-reeking second floor with its incoherent shouts. But two old women with sense and character survive in it, thanks to a caliber of friendship rare in the world of youth and health.

Mrs. Cross and Mrs. Kidd have known each other for more than seventy-five years. A valuable feature of this story is the care taken to explain the women's contrasting pasts: their schoolgirl personalities, their parents, their educations, their families. All of this individualizes the two women, who are anything but types. Thus Mrs. Kidd, the educated one, keeps science displays on her bedroom shelf. Mrs. Cross, the extrovert, busies herself in visiting old and new friends in the home, especially in attending to the inarticulate stroke victim, Jack. The differences between the two women also define the unique attraction between them, part critical, part caring.

The crisis of the story is the tantrum thrown by Jack in eventually rejecting the kindly guidance of Mrs. Cross. In doing so, Jack is spurning the imaginative tenderness of the old woman in favor of the dim attractions of Charlotte, a younger but silly woman. Mrs. Cross is crushed; she "felt her heart give a big flop. Her heart was like an old crippled crow, flopping about in her chest." Then Mrs. Kidd shows an equal tenderness by seeing her friend safely to her room at the cost of her own exhaustion.

This story also displays the difficulties that adult children may have in grasping the present identity of their aged parents. Mrs. Kidd's children "want her fixed where she was forty or fifty years ago, these children who are aging themselves."

242 *Author:* Nightingale, J. David

Title: "The Nursing Home." In **Love Is Ageless: Stories about Alzheimer's Disease.** Ed. by Jessica Bryan. Oakland, Calif.: Serala Pr., 1987

Genre: story

Commentary: The story recreates the agonizing experience of an adult son's last visit to his mother, a woman in her eighties who suffers from an advanced stage of Alzheimer's disease. Their interaction illustrates the anxiety and frustration involved in trying to communicate with the severely demented. The story also reveals the anguish of a family member who sees his parent reduced to an incoherent cipher.

The narrator comments, "The sons who had been exiled to boarding school by the age of seven had now exiled their own mother." The old woman's place of exile is a nursing home in her native England. She is surrounded by women who are experiencing serious physical and mental decline. The son's visit is a series of awkward moments, near disasters, and dead ends. When the son tries to converse with his mother, his attempts are met by repeated nonsequiturs and incoherent references to the past. This 1925 graduate of London University is now reduced to someone who doesn't know where she is, doesn't recognize her son, doesn't know her husband's name, can't add three and four, and has to wear a diaper.

On leaving, the son feels resigned to the terms of this unresolvable mother-son relationship. He sits on a plane headed for New York City and takes out a picture of his mother as a young bridesmaid at her sister's wedding. He describes her "pretty brown curls—smart figure—bright eyes." He recalls showing her the picture the day before: "Although Mother denied it, it was in fact her."

243 *Author:* Norris, Leslie

Title: "My Uncle's Story." In **The Atlantic Monthly,** 246:55–61 (Nov. 1980)

Genre: story

Commentary: This story, which records a young man's memories of his uncle's experiences in Wales after World War I, illustrates how circumstances can break a person's spirit and destroy the prospects for a fulfilling old age. It also reveals how little the young may understand of the hardships and disappointments faced by the old.

The nephew's earliest memories of his uncle are of a vibrant, adventurous young man who joined the Army at 16, fought in France, and then returned home to work in the mines. The nephew loved to hear the story of the time his uncle and a friend spent a drunken two nights holed up in a cave near town. Rescued by a search party, the two men came back to the village "like returned warriors, like heroes."

When the mines are shut down during the Depression, the uncle leaves home to look for work. Still the nephew responds to what he envisions as the romance of his uncle's life. He imagines the adventures his uncle must be having as he walks the "Great North Road" across England. Several years later, when the uncle returns home, his nephew is surprised to find that the man he had supposed would be a swashbuckling adventurer is now an old man who sits silently and forlornly in the corner of the room.

One day when the nephew is a teenager, he finally asks the old man, "What was it like when you were a tramp?" This question prompts the uncle to tell the story of his hard life on the road. The nephew recalls feeling overwhelmed by the tragedy and hopelessness of this story.

244 *Author:* Oates, Joyce Carol
     Title: "A Theory of Knowledge." In **Night-Side: Eighteen Tales.**
        New York: Vanguard, 1977
     Genre: story
     Commentary: Oates' story suggests that the very old and the very young have a great deal in common. Both are fragile beings, whose security and peace of mind utterly depend on their caregivers. The story illustrates what terrible consequences can occur when a person is ignored and abandoned. At the same time, it demonstrates that sometimes acts of courage are required of the person—at no matter what age—to rekindle loving and sensitive human relationships.

Professor Weber, 77, languishes in retirement in the mountains in upstate New York in the 1890s. Ostensibly he is working on his crowning achievement as a philosopher—a book called *A Theory of Knowledge.* In reality he spends his days engaged in an intense and bitter life review. Then he befriends a young boy who seems attracted to the old man. The boy is silent, wary, and dressed in ragged clothes. To Weber the boy is a respite from his daughter's patronizing caregiving.

For some time Weber suspects that the boy is being abused by his parents, but his daughter belittles his concerns. The climax of the story occurs when the professor Weber acts on his convictions and tries to rescue the boy from his parents. He overcomes extraordinary physical obstacles to free the boy, who clearly *has* been abused by his parents, and the story ends abruptly just when the rescue is completed.

Although Weber's life has been devoted to philosophy, his system of philosophy is abstract and out of touch with the ambiguities of real life. The ending of the story portrays him acting on a new theory of knowledge, one that places actions before abstractions. Professor Weber responds with his feelings to the boy's sufferings, and their interaction is a lesson in how love redeems hopeless and desperate lives.

245 *Author:* O'Connor, Flannery
Title: "The Artificial Nigger" (1955). In **The Complete Stories of Flannery O'Connor.** New York: Farrar, 1971
Genre: story
Commentary: This tragicomic story centers on the love-hate relationship between a grandfather and grandson as they visit a big city (Atlanta) where both are strangers. Mr. Head, a sixtyish rural widower, fondly believes that age has blessed him with "that calm understanding of life that makes him a suitable guide for the young." Nelson, the orphaned grandson who lives with him, "was never satisfied until he had given an impudent answer." So the two board the train, each trying to outpoint and downgrade the other.

Their day in Atlanta produces one mishap and one argument after the other until a climactic embarrassment overtakes them. The boy, running away in panic, knocks down an old woman and attracts a crowd of indignant passersby. Mr. Head, on catching up, is so frightened and ashamed that he denies knowing his grandson. A horrid silence falls between the two as he wanders on with the boy following. For the first time in his life, the old man feels spiritually lost, damned, denied salvation. Grace descends on him when they pass an "artificial nigger," a plaster figure about which Mr. Head is inspired to make a simple joke about city tastes. The tension breaks. The boy is relieved; the grandfather feels God's forgiveness.

246 *Title:* "A Late Encounter with the Enemy" (1953)
Commentary: The folly of prizing immortality is hilariously enacted in this tale of Civil War veteran "General" Tennessee Flintlock Sash, aged 104, a vain and thoroughly addled star of parades and stage appearances. Probably once a foot soldier, the "General" has

reached extreme old age as little more than a picturesque doll. "The past and the future were the same thing to him, one forgotten and the other not remembered; he had no more notion of dying than a cat." He lives mainly to be exhibited on ceremonial occasions, notably a movie premier in Atlanta twelve years previous when much was made of him.

Now his sixtyish granddaughter, Sally Poker, cherishes his attendance at her belated graduation from college. There he makes his final appearance and, as corpse, his final exit.

Two other stories show the pain that a settled older person can feel on being uprooted from a familiar culture (the South) and planted in a daughter's home in a strange city (New York): "The Geranium" (1946) and an elaborate reworking of the same situation, "Judgment Day" (circa 1964, posthumous).

247 *Author:* Olsen, Tillie
   Title: "Tell Me a Riddle." In **Tell Me a Riddle: A Collection by Tillie Olsen.** Philadelphia: Lippincott, 1961
   Genre: story
   Commentary: Eva, a bitter, passionate old Jewish woman, dying of cancer, reflects on a life as wife and mother whose vitality has been squeezed out by the demands of children, husband, poverty. How life-long conflicts can surface in the confusion of terminal fatigue is compellingly shown in this long story.

Eva's husband wants to sell their house and move to the old folks' haven maintained by his lodge in Florida. He wants to be free of house care and to be with congenial friends. Eva refuses. She has a craving for solitude: *"Never again to be forced to move to the rhythms of others."* He argues with her repeatedly; she responds with obstinate brevity. One senses both her deep rebellion against his masculine self-centeredness, and the old passions and habits that still lock them into a common orbit.

Growing in sympathy, her husband takes her to their children's homes, where she responds only minimally to demands on her grandmotherly attention. Finally they go to Los Angeles, where she is wonderfully ministered to by her granddaughter, Jeannie, a nurse. In memory Eva relives the turbulent life that has formed her: childhood in Russia; her humanistic education by Lisa, a Tolstoyan idealist; her youthful utopianism; prison; the days of young love; the music in her life, especially that of her native village. As the story ends she is on her deathbed, hearing that childhood music, tended lovingly by the husband who never understood her and by Jeannie who does.

The title comes from her grandchildren's request: "Tell me a riddle, Grammy." "I know no riddles" (meaning perhaps that life has been such a terrible enigma that nursery riddles have no meaning).

The narrative technique is characterized by streams of Eva's thoughts; scraps of dialogue; quotation fragments; wisps of memory. The effect is to bring Eva's introspective isolation directly into the reader's experience.

248 *Author:* Potter, Nancy

Title: "A Short Vacation" (1986). In **Legacies.** Champaign: Univ. of Illinois Pr., 1987

Genre: story

Commentary: When Ned Smith, recently widowed, returns from the hospital after recovering from a fall at home, he sets out to change his life. Ned's wife dominated him during their marriage of sixty years. During his recovery at home Ned muses. "It seemed. . . that he had spent such a long time being old that he had not properly grown up at all." Now that he is free of his wife's tyranny, the rest of his life will be a "short vacation" that he can enjoy on his own terms.

Early in this process of self-renewal and adaptation, he meets Olympia, an elderly widow who delivers his Meals-on-Wheels lunch. When he learns that this is her first day on the job, he volunteers to ride along and help her find the other addresses on the route. Soon they become a team: she drives and he makes the deliveries. Then they begin to eat lunch together and share their life stories. Ned appreciates Olympia, because she is a good listener and she makes him feel that "life was sweeter than he could admit to anyone, even to himself."

"A Private Space" (1984) portrays an older couple's dysfunctional marriage. Sid Crane's wife tyrannizes him relentlessly. She controls all aspects of their life together. He tries to find a measure of independence apart from her by renting a small box at the post office. One day he arrives at the post office and finds a note tucked in the box. The note, apparently from his wife, warns him to "watch your step." Now the entrapment is complete, and Sid is left feeling hopelessness and despair.

249 *Author:* Rosner, Anne F.
   Title: "Prize Tomatoes" (1981). In **Best American Short Stories, 1982**. Ed. by John Gardner and Shannon Ravenel. Boston: Houghton, 1982
   Genre: story
   Commentary: The rebellion of an aged father against an over-protective daughter makes the story of Walter Brinkman, retired business leader. He has given his grown children much to worry about since his attempted suicide over the death of his wife. On his recovery, his daughter Barbara and family have moved into his house to keep a close eye on him.
   When Walter takes an obsessive new interest in a ham radio friend, his family takes such alarm that he leaves that interest for still another, gardening. Again, his family and psychiatrist take fright. They even begrudge him the privacy to study seed catalogs. What his family is missing throughout is that Walter has grown into a different person from the dynamic businessman they thought they knew. His unhappy Barbara, so bent on restoring an outdated image of her father, shows how close to cruelty the misguided supervision of an aged parent can come.
   The rest of the story carries Walter into a successful revolt. He escapes in part by riding the bus, where he shares his difficulties with Mason Miggs, a black man also misunderstood by his children. He evades the campaign to get him back to his business career. He continues to garden, and in a climactic episode breaks away from Barbara to get to a fair where he finds that his tomatoes (and he) have won the blue ribbon.

250 *Author:* Rossiter, Sarah
   Title: "Civil War." In **Beyond This Bitter Air**. Champaign: Univ. of Illinois Pr., 1987
   Genre: story
   Commentary: After Eliot Jarvis, 89, suffers a stroke, his daughter Louise, a professional photographer, decides to hire a live-in companion for him so that she can return to work. Their choice is Sue Ellen, a lively, sensitive, and assertive young woman of 29, who turns out to be the perfect companion for Eliot. The two soon establish an invigorating routine that leads to Eliot's physical rejuvenation and fosters the resolution of a longstanding feud between him and his daughter.
   Louise is concerned that Sue Ellen lacks credentials for working with the elderly. For example, Eliot constantly refers to the Civil War in his conversations with his daughter. Louise attributes this

speech pattern to advancing dementia, and she thinks Sue Ellen lacks the skills to deal with such a complex medical condition.

But after Sue Ellen is hired and Louise leaves her father's Florida home, the old man's physical health begins to improve. Sue Ellen is determined to help Eliot walk again. Her goal is that he will walk across the street to the ocean. As she encourages him, she begins to gain his confidence. He begins to share some of his fears about physical decline.

The source of Louise's alienation from Eliot is her late mother, who was a ruthless, domineering woman. Her mother's attempts to teach Louise to be the perfect child served only to constrain the young girl's emotional development. In reality, both Louise and her father had spontaneous and adventurous spirits, but their lives were regimented and inhibited by this woman's devotion to inflexible rules. Eliot never loved his wife. His references to the "civil war" are actually to his conflict with his wife and his alienation from his daughter. At the end of the story, Sue Ellen succeeds in her mission: Eliot, using two canes, crosses the street, stands on the beach, and shouts, "We've won." When Louise discovers them there, she snaps their picture and realizes that now she can begin to overcome her mother's bitter legacy.

In "Star Light, Star Bright," a young woman, Lucy, visits her grandmother, who is suffering from the advanced stages of Alzheimer's disease. The only way Lucy can converse with the old woman without agitating her is to pretend to be a replacement for her regular attendant. In this way Lucy discovers a way to talk to her grandmother: she tells the old woman about her family and about the grandmother she lived with when she was a child. She tells the old woman her grandmother and she used to wish upon a star each night. She repeats "Star light, star bright. . . ," but the old woman doesn't join in the refrain. Although Lucy is forced to admit her grandmother's condition is irreversible, she gains some comfort in expressing some of her long-repressed feelings about how important her grandmother was to her.

251 *Author:* Salloum, Vicki
  Title: "Sitty Victoria." In **When I Am an Old Woman I Shall Wear Purple: An Anthology of Short Stories and Poetry.** Ed. by Sandra Martz. Manhattan Beach, Calif.: Papier-Maché Pr., 1987
  Genre: story
  Commentary: This story is an epic portrait of a great old woman, Sitty Victoria, a Lebanese immigrant over 100 years old. She has

lived heroically in the United States and is now about to be placed in an "Asylum for the Aged" because, as her remaining daughter explains, "I'm over eighty. I can't care for her no more."

The narrator, Sitty's granddaughter by parents long dead, feels strong compassion for the ancient woman and wants to stay home from college to care for her. When her aunt Alma sternly directs her to resume her education, she goes in to Sitty Victoria to explain what must be. In her own mind she reviews what this woman has lived through: coming alone from her native Beirut, marrying in New Orleans, running a dry goods store with her husband, Jiddy. After he committed suicide at the outbreak of the Depression, Sitty worked "like a dog" to pay off the creditors and to raise their eleven children in the big high-ceilinged house nearby.

Now the narrator's beloved Sitty is frail, worn, decrepit, sitting in her daughter's home with a strange oblivion awaiting her. The narrator hears hurricane warnings on the radio. Instead of boarding up the house, she stays by Sitty, trying to tell her what's ahead. The old woman sweetly embraces the granddaughter, then shakes off the young woman's help as she walks with "incandescent eyes" into the storm, strikes out for the big house of so much family history, and collapses in death.

252 *Author:* Sayles, John
    Title: "At the Anarchists' Convention." In **The Atlantic Monthly,**
       243:48–52 (Feb. 1979)
    Genre: story
    Commentary: In this lighthearted story, Sayles creates a memorable gallery of characters who have never forgotten the legacy of their days of protest. The "Anarchists' Convention" is the annual reunion in New York City of a group of anarchists who were active in the 1920s and 30s. In old age these characters continue to defy authority, to hold old grudges and longstanding feuds, and to resist any form of regimentation of thought or action.

In some ways the story is a satiric view of old age; lofty philosophical disputes soon degenerate into petty squabbles. (Imagine anarchists even *having* a convention!) At the same time these old people are admirable because they maintain high levels of energy and vitality, hold longstanding affections, and are determined to act in concert once they have defined a common foe. Their most common bond is the "raw-throated sound, a grating, insistent sound, a sound born out of all the insults swallowed, the battles lost, out of all the smothered dreams and desires. . . the sound of a terrible deep despair." Set against the pain of their losses and the memories of oppression that haunt them is the renewal that occurs every time they are confronted with oppression.

Leo Gold, the narrator, has returned to the convention after two years' absence. The highlight of his reunion is to see Sophie, the woman he has always loved. But seeing Sophie is the source of pain because she married one of Leo's arch foes in the movement, a man named Brinkman. At dinner the speaker honors the memory of Brinkman, who died the year before. Leo recalls the man affectionately, despite the longstanding feud between them.

Then the hotel manager comes in to announce that the hotel has booked the anarchists into the wrong room. The Rotary Club from Sioux Falls is supposed to have their space. But instead of passive acceptance the manager encounters active resistance. When he threatens to call the police, all of the anarchists respond as one—"like the twinge of a single nerve"—and they act in concert to resist this echo of an old oppression. Leo characterizes the moment this way: "Like a shot of adrenaline, I feel fifty again! Sophie, . . . it was always so good just to be at your side!" At the end of the story, the old anarchists have erected barricades to keep the oppressors out of their room.

253   *Author:* Scofield, Sandra
Title: "Loving Leo." In **Women and Aging: An Anthology by Women.** Ed. by Jo Alexander and others. Corvallis, Ore.: Calyx, 1986
Genre: story
Commentary: Greta Boll, a tough but poetic widow, wonders whether to enter a late marriage. At 65, she has had a hard life: farm worker, railroad cook, flour packer, rest-home worker. Her personal life has been marked by "scattered and lost menfolk, ungrateful children, . . . despots, bumblers, liars, and thieves." Yet she has made a better life for her family, she has good memories of her husband and grandparents, and she loves to harvest the sweet-scented apricots ripening in her Texas backyard.

Leo Clark, a nearly blind old man whom she had met in the rest home, has been after her for half a year. "I can see the girl under your belly fat," he tells her. He is tender. He is confident. He will be a good provider. He will share his interests and learn hers. Something in Greta responds: "something wild, young, long ago given up for dead." But she cannot quite give up her old life. "She needs her privacy and the company of ghosts."

This fine portrait ends enigmatically with Greta quietly enjoying the taste of her apricots.

254 *Author:* Shacochis, Bob
   Title: "Where Pelham Fell" (1985). In **The Next New World.** New
      York: Crown, 1988
   Genre: story
   Commentary: This story illustrates the consequences of one old
   man's obsession with the meaning of the past. Colonel Coates, retired from the Army Corps of Engineers, has long adored the ideals
   of the Confederacy, the pure image of rebellion, the noble sacrifices
   made by fallen heroes. His wife, frustrated with his unremitting devotion to the Southern cause, often had wished he would "vanish
   into history, which was what the man had always wanted anyway."
      One day Colonel Coates, afflicted with advancing signs of de-
   mentia, goes for a drive through countryside that was once the site
   of battlefields. When he passes a highway marker commemorating
   the death of Major John Pelham, who fought for the Confederate
   Army in Virginia and who died on the battlefield nearby, Colonel
   Coates decides to locate the exact spot where the Major fell. This
   whimsical journey culminates in his joining the ranks of the fallen
   heroes of his beloved Confederacy.
      Although the Colonel never discovers where Pelham fell, he re-
   turns home triumphant after a chance encounter with an old black
   man, who turns over to him the remains of Confederate soldiers
   plowed up when the land was cleared in 1867. This "inheritance"
   changes Colonel Coates' life. He dedicates his life to the discovery of
   the soldiers' identities. Eventually he unravels the mystery of the
   bones, and he appears to be on the verge of identifying the soldiers'
   regiment when he dies of a heart attack after feeling overwhelmed
   by the presence of the spirits of all of the soldiers from the regiment.

   Another story in this collection treats themes related to aging. In
   "Celebrations of the New World" (1985), a family reunion is the setting for revelations about the effects of Alzheimer's disease on family members. The narrator's interaction with two brothers, both of
   whom suffer from the disease, illustrates the importance of respect-
   ing the individuality of persons with Alzheimer's disease.

255 *Author:* Singer, Isaac Bashevis
   Title: "Old Love" (1975). In **The Collected Stories of Isaac Bashevis
   Singer.** Trans. by Saul Bellow and others. New York: Farrar,
   1982
   Genre: story
   Commentary: Here is a tragic but beautiful story of the possibilities
   of new love in the late years. Harry Bendiner, 82, rich, three times a

widower, is living a lonely, apprehensive life in his Miami Beach condominium when the doorbell announces his next-door neighbor, Ethel Brokeles. As they chat, a miracle of resurrection occurs for this deadened old man.

Ethel is younger and physically attractive to him ("Harry cast glances at her round knees"). She had loved an older husband and tells Harry, "I always liked a man to be older than me." She and Harry share a Polish Jewish culture. They have both thrived financially. One can understand Harry's feeling that "heaven had acceded to his secret desires."

Something of a call to new life has reached Ethel, too. On the death of her husband she had fallen mentally ill. Her husband, she reports, was "calling me from the grave." Then Harry appeared, ready to fill the void.

Within the day of meeting, Harry and Ethel engage to marry. At once the new life fades. Ethel "had undergone a startling transformation. . . . Her face had grown pale, shrunken, and aged." Her suicide that night tells Harry that she has answered her dead husband's call after all. Harry sinks back into the moribund mood she had found him in.

This late opening into love has not entirely shut off. The old man conceives "an adventurous idea"—to find Ethel's daughter in the Canadian wilderness, and be a father to her, and try with her to understand human frailty.

Two other stories from the same volume treat the trials and potentials of old age. In "The Spinoza of Market Street" (1961), laid in pre–World War I Warsaw, an aged Jewish philosopher and a spinster peddler form a friendship that evolves into marriage. "Grandfather and Grandson" (1971), set in Warsaw in the same era, shows the conflict between a devout old Jew and his revolutionary grandson as a trial of the old man's faith.

256 *Author:* Steinbeck, John
Title: "The Leader of the People" (1937). In **The Short Novels of John Steinbeck.** New York: Viking, 1953
Genre: story
Commentary: To describe the achievements of one's life would seem to be one of the delights of old age. How these delights can be enjoyed without tiring the listeners is the question raised in this story of the boy Jody and his grandfather.

Grandfather was once "leader of the people." He had led a wagon train west in frontier days—a classic exploit in the American drive to master the new continent. Over and over he tells of the Indians, the hunger, the drought of that western journey, until he has bored many of his listeners, especially his son-in-law Carl Tiflin, whose family he has come to visit at their California ranch.

Wearied out of patience, Carl complains bitterly to the family just as Grandfather enters the room the next morning. The moment is awful, not to be dispelled by Carl's anguished apology. But the little grandson, Jody, has felt enormous excitement at Grandfather's tales and goes to keep company with the saddened old man on the porch. "I tell these old stories," says Grandfather, "but they're not what I want to tell. I only know how I want people to feel when I tell them." The story ends with a touching gesture of affection from the little boy.

The story is especially poignant through being told from the point of view of a warm-hearted boy who is sensitive and vulnerable to the moods of his elders.

The time is probably early in the century, when some of the old pioneers still survived, hating the Pacific Ocean "because it stopped them," as Grandfather explains. When he laments to Jody that "westering has died out of the people," he voices a grief often felt by the aged, over the vanishing of values that inspirited their youth.

257 *Author:* Stern, Richard
Title: "Dr. Cahn's Visit." In **The Atlantic Monthly,** 244:80–82 (Oct. 1979)
Genre: story
Commentary: Dr. Cahn, 91, who suffers from the advanced stages of Alzheimer's disease, is brought to the hospital by his son to visit his wife, who is near death from cancer. The son believes that although the old man probably will not recognize his wife, the visit should be made because "they have been the center of each other's lives." But the visit surprises everyone. For a few moments lucidity returns to Dr. Cahn, and his wife and he interact meaningfully. Then the old man's clarity of mind departs as suddenly as it had brightened. The visit is over, and the old man and his son return home.

The story illustrates how one's neat expectations of life can be overturned by circumstances and fate. Everyone had thought that Dr. Cahn, eleven years older than his wife, would be the first to die. Everyone in the family had expected that the planned last visit would be meaningless. The story also illuminates the strains experienced by caregivers, who are overwhelmed by the needs of Alzheimer's victims.

There is a lesson for the son, too, as he interacts with his dying mother. In the hospital he gains an insight into his mother's character. He experiences her courage, defiance, even rage at the suffering inflicted on her by cancer and by the harsh treatments that are required by her doctors. He characterizes her look as one of "human beauty" as he compares her to a fine work of art, and he describes her voice as "rusty, avian" and "beautiful."

258 *Author:* Swift, Jonathan
  Title: [The Immortal Struldbruggs], Part II, Chapter 10 of **Gulliver's
    Travels** (1726)
  Genre: story
  Commentary: The folly of wanting to live forever is brilliantly shown in this section of Swift's great satiric fantasy. Merely staying alive is not the same, it appears, as living well; death in extreme old age is a release rather than a doom.

Captain Lemuel Gulliver sails to strange countries in which human foibles appear in exaggerated perspective. When he visits the kingdom of Luggnagg, he is told of certain citizens, the Struldbruggs, who never die. These immortal beings, it seems, are born rarely and at random among the population, and, at present, number only in the hundreds.

Gulliver is surprised and delighted to learn that immortality is actually granted to these favored beings, though none of them is immediately present. On being asked what he himself would do with immortal life, Gulliver expatiates grandly: He would first become rich, then master the arts and sciences, then become the historian and advisor to his nation. He and his fellow immortals would educate the young in public and private virtue, etc., etc.

When the laughter of his listeners dies down, Gulliver is informed about the actual nature and condition of the Struldbruggs. They do not live in perpetual youth, as Gulliver had supposed. They age like all other humans, acquiring their share of vices and disability. "When they came to fourscore years . . . , they had not only all the follies and infirmities of other old men, but many more which arose from the dreadful prospect of never dying. They were not only opinionative, peevish, covetous, morose, vain, talkative; but uncapable of friendship, and dead to all natural affection . . . . Envy and impotent desires are their prevailing passions." They quickly forget their vocabulary, nor can they read, "because their memory will not serve to carry them from the beginning of a sentence to the end." The Struldbruggs' best fortune, it seems is to succumb to senile dementia in which they no longer know their own misery.

259 *Author:* Taylor, Peter
     Title: "Porte-Cochère" (1949). In **The Widows of Thornton.** New
         York: Harcourt, 1954
     Genre: story
     Commentary: Seldom has fiction shown in such concentration the
     stresses of a morbid family pattern—the toxic blends of rage and af-
     fection, of doting and demanding, of rebellion and surrender—as in
     Taylor's portrait of this old widower and his children.
        Old Ben Brantley, 76 and nearly blind, is a despotic father whose
     adult children have traveled to Nashville to celebrate his birthday.
     His special favorite is his son Clifford, whose affection he aches for.
     But he quarrels violently with Clifford for avoiding a chat before the
     birthday dinner.
        His unfolding story shows Ben as once a frightened boy cruelly
     beaten by his father, resolving to "go away to another country"
     when he grows up, later resolving never to beat or restrain his own
     children. But as Old Ben, he has never left his boyhood home after
     all. Though he has given his children freedom from physical beat-
     ing, he has imposed the subtler and far more oppressive tyranny of
     constant surveillance (from his study above the porte-cochère or
     "drive-under") and constant expectation of being coddled.
        Clifford, in whom he has invested such pride and fondness, has
     become an alien who can tell him with steely clarity: "Whenever in
     your life have you been anything but [childish]? There's not a senile
     bone in your brain. It's your children that have got old, and you've
     stayed young—and not in any good sense, Papa, only in a bad one!
     You play sly games with us still or you quarrel with us. What the
     hell do you want of us, Papa?" As the day closes on the old man's
     birthday, what should have been a day of patriarchal celebration
     ends with Old Ben reverting to his own father's rage as he whips the
     chairs in the darkness of his locked study, calling them by his chil-
     dren's names.

260 *Author:* Thomas, Annabel
     Title: "Ashur and Evir." In **The Phototropic Woman.** Iowa City:
         Univ. of Iowa Pr., 1981
     Genre: story
     Commentary: How to balance security and adventure in the late
     years is the theme of this affectionate conflict between brother and
     sister. Ashur, a dairy farmer, is selling the farm and investing his
     share of the proceeds into permanent care at a retirement home.
     What he is really doing is to convert a life's work into a guarantee of

security. He has taken a fierce pride in that work, but a fire that had once nearly destroyed their home has scarred Ashur with an anxious temperament lacking any sense of daring for the time ahead.

His older sister, Evir, by contrast, is happy in that most insecure of occupations, giving piano lessons. To Ashur's impatience, she will not commit her share of the money to the home. At her last students' recital, Evir is seen radiant in the music-making she loves best. She ends the evening by happily deciding to rent a room in town and continue giving lessons to the students whose life she has touched.

261 *Author:* Tisdale, Sallie

Title: "Dancing in the Wind." In **Love Is Ageless: Stories about Alzheimer's Disease**. Ed. by Jessica Bryan. Oakland, Calif.: Serala Pr., 1987

Genre: story

Commentary: This story offers the point of view of "a part-time charge nurse in an old, not very good, urban nursing home." The narrator relates objectively and without sentimentality her experiences with the old and the demented. Despite the unpredictability of her interactions and the often desperate conditions of the patients, the nurse is fulfilled by her job. She feels "a measure of peace here, a sense of belonging." She appreciates the straightforward terms of employment: "the responsibility is mine, the consequences are mine." She views her job as "a labor of love," but she is careful to define that "love" as a form of compassion for the old people she serves. She explains, "I let them do their own suffering."

The nurse sympathizes with families who are shocked by the bizarre behaviors associated with Alzheimer's disease. But she reminds us that—in spite of these behaviors—most old people are not consumed by self-pity, pain, or suffering. She also provides insights into how she and other staff members in the nursing home maintain a balance between sensitivity and professionalism.

Tisdale shows us old age and the effects of Alzheimer's disease vividly and honestly. If we don't flinch, we see Maud, who is "eighty-six years old and weighs just that many pounds. She is nearly bald; her thin fine white-grey hair has been rubbed nearly away by all her years in bed." Then there is the old woman who was continually falling out of her chair, even after repeatedly being restrained. One day the nurse stood over her and lamented, "What am I going to do with you?" From the floor the old woman answered, "Don't stop trying, dear."

262 *Author:* Tolstoy, Leo
Title: "The Death of Ivan Ilyich" (1886).
Genre: story
Commentary: This account of the illness and spiritual struggle of a
Russian bureaucrat in the 1880s so powerfully translates to American upper-middle-class culture that the differences in century and
nation seem trivial. Even the fact that its protagonist, Ivan Ilyich, is
only in his forties seems a technicality. Here is a mature man, at the
top of his profession, father of a married daughter, stricken with
disability when he had expected life to go on pleasantly and indefinitely. The ordeal is not uncommon among aging persons still active
in a career.

The story opens with Ivan's wake and funeral service—a cutting
satire of the callous hypocrisy with which so many people treat the
death of others. The survivors reflect complacently, "It is he who is
dead and not I." The widow complains not of her husband's suffering but of her own. The others conjecture what promotions will
result from the vacancy created by Ivan's death. They arrange bridge
for later. . . .

Then Tolstoy reviews Ivan's life, which "had been most simple
and most ordinary and therefore most terrible." Ivan was born into a
bureaucratic family. He studied law and entered the provincial civil
service. As an elegant young gentleman ("yuppy" would be a rough
contemporary equivalent), he enjoyed the society and night life. On
succeeding promotions and transfers, he gradually refined his performance of duty into an exact and cold but satisfying routine. He
married well as was expected but soon tired of his wife's demands
for attention and gradually withdrew into his career. A final promo-
tion, seized for its salary alone, brought him to his high point.

The ominous refrain throughout this review is that "Everything
was as it should be." Everything was pleasant, fitting, exactly right
for a successful careerist. A slight accident on redecorating his new
home, a slip from a stepladder, transforms gradually into something
like a deadly cancer, its pain constantly thrusting into the serene life
Ivan wants to continue.

As he becomes aware that death, not recovery, is his reality, Ivan
also finds that everyone around him, even the doctors, has reduced
him to a routine just as he had reduced others. They lie about the
oncoming death; they conspire to keep him from facing it. Only his
small son and the peasant servant, Gerasim, treat him humanely as
a dying man needing comfort. The deathbed scene, in which Ivan finally reaches the truth of his life and death, is strongly moving.

263 *Author:* Trevor, William
  Title: "Broken Homes" (1978). In **The Stories of William Trevor.**
    New York: Penguin, 1983
  Genre: story
  Commentary: The appalling damage that insensitive "charity" can
  inflict on the helpless old is portrayed in Trevor's account of an 87-
  year-old London widow being "helped" against her will.

  Mrs. Malby has lived contentedly above a greengrocer's shop.
  Though her husband died five years ago and her two sons in World
  War II, she has come to terms with her bereavement and wishes only
  to live on serenely in her sunlit apartment. A shy individualist, she
  dreads being some day forced by senility to live with other old people. Accordingly she is anxious to understand what others tell her,
  to avoid betraying incapacity by any sign.

  This contentment is fractured one day when a teacher appears
  from a nearby comprehensive school (where nonselective standards
  admit delinquent and homeless children). He informs Mrs. Malby
  that her kitchen is to be decorated by the students free of charge "to
  foster a deeper understanding between the generations." Fearing to
  appear difficult, she fails to ward off his project.

  A nightmare begins on the appointed day as the student-
  decorators appear: three teenage boys and a girl, all in blue jeans.
  They cheerfully call her by the wrong name; they turn up the radio;
  they smoke cigarettes. Though she begs them simply to wash the
  walls, they begin sloshing yellow paint on walls and carpet. Later
  Mrs. Malby enters her bedroom to find the girl and a boy having
  sex, the air rank with sweat, her pet birds flopping about. Though
  her friend the greengrocer chases out the children and partly cleans
  up the mess, the rape of her little world has been complete. The
  teacher who unleashed it is called back. Unrepentant, he dabs fu-
  tilely at the stained carpet, telling the sweet old lady that he was
  only "trying to make the world a better place" for kids from broken
  homes.

264 *Title:* "Attracta" (1978)
  Commentary: Here is a moving account of a generously heroic older
  woman. Attracta, an aging Irish Protestant schoolteacher, learns of
  the atrocious murder of a former student at the hands of terrorists.
  She herself had lost her parents by a mistaken ambush (intended for
  British soldiers), but has grown up receiving affectionate, expiatory
  attention from the man and housekeeper who had laid the plot. She

now tries to explain to her pupils what such atrocities mean, how the criminals may become decent, how God still has mercy. The pupils are merely confused and report the talk to their parents, who in turn complain to the archdeacon, who decides that retirement time has come for Attracta. She accepts, without loss of faith.

Two other stories deserve attention. "The General's Day" (1967) shows the pathetic bumbling of an old military hero trying to retaste his pleasure-seeking years. His final tearful whisper: "My God Almighty, I could live for twenty years." "The Paradise Lounge" (1981) contrasts young love and old love, with special attention to a lovely eightyish woman who all her life had loved an unattainable married man.

265 *Author:* Updike, David
     Title: "Indian Summer" (1983). In **Out on the Marsh: Stories by David Updike.** Boston: Godine, 1988
     Genre: story
     Commentary: While visiting his grandmother, a young man learns how much resolution and even courage may be required of an old person. His grandmother, widowed several years earlier, has attained a sense of wholeness, serenity, and peace in her rural environment. She has maintained the farm by herself, and she has surrounded herself with animals—a horse, a dog, about twenty cats, and wild birds. At the same time, she is aware that her existence there is finite. She is experiencing symptoms of physical decline, she is wary of the coming winter, and she is fearful of impending changes. How long can she hold on? What will happen to the farm when she dies? The story reveals that old people like the boy's grandmother, who live alone, face an ever-present tension based on the demands of the natural and social environments.

Her neighbors have advised her to get rid of all of the animals. She tells her grandson, "They think the animals tire me out. It's *they* who tire me out." An incident in the story bears out her complaint. While feeding the animals one evening, the young man and his grandmother discover a nest of kittens in the barn. One of the neighbors, thinking that the old woman will raise them, has dropped them off. But the kittens are ill with distemper, and the old woman realizes that although she would love to raise them, she lacks the resources to take care of them. She resents being taken advantage of in this way. She tells her grandson, "You'd think it was simple for an old woman to live alone in the middle of nowhere, but not this grandma." At the end of the story, the young man returns from a long walk and learns that his grandmother has killed the kittens. He respects the hard choice she has had to make.

266 *Author:* Vivante, Arturo
Title: "The Soft Core" (1972). In **Run to the Waterfall.** New York: Scribner, 1979
Genre: story
Commentary: A middle-aged son recounts his ambivalent feelings toward his 80-year-old father, who is recuperating from a stroke suffered six months before. Giacomo characterizes his father as a self-centered, willful, single-minded, and arrogant old man who is insensitive to his son's need for affection and love. When the old man experiences another physical attack, Giacomo worries that his father will die before their relationship can be resolved.

Giacomo respects and fears his father, but he does not love him. Giacomo wants most of all to escape his father's stern will. He survives the stress of this hurtful relationship by constructing in his mind an image of the old man as an ideal father figure, someone who is sweet and worthy of admiration and respect. The reality is that Giacomo is psychologically disabled by his father. He feels suffocated by the old man's domineering attitude. Each time the son tries to renew their relationship, the old man dashes his hopes.

At the end of the story, Giacomo works patiently and sensitively to help his father recover from his momentary mental confusion. The old man responds warmly to his son's attention. Giacomo feels comfortable talking to his father for the first time in years. Giacomo realizes that "he was reaching the secret, soft core" in his father. He was uncovering his father's true self, his youthful self, that the old man had buried over the years with selfish preoccupations and an unyielding temperament. Although Giacomo knows that his father will soon recover his memory and revert to his former behavior, Giacomo is satisfied that this communion has given him a measure of the resolution he has always needed.

Vivante shows the same father-son relationship in another way in "At the Dinner Table" (1974) from the same volume. Here Giacomo dreads the inclusion of his ailing father at the dinner table with other guests. The old man's conversational gambits are too predictable, he thinks, his mannerisms too eccentric. But the guests find a winning charm in all this, enough to transform the son's embarrassment into positive pleasure in his parent.

267 *Author:* Vonnegut, Kurt, Jr.
Title: "Tomorrow and Tomorrow and Tomorrow." In **Welcome to the Monkey House: A Collection of Short Works by Kurt Vonnegut, Jr.** New York: Delacorte, 1968.
Genre: story
Commentary: People who predict a senior boom early in the next century will find a provocative projection in this ghoulish little fantasy. In 2158, the life span has extended indefinitely, thanks to medical science and especially to a wonder drug called "anti-gerasone." Em and Lou Schwartz, the main characters, are 112 years old and 93, respectively. In spite of longevity, life has remained at least as drab as our own plastic culture has made it. Overcrowding is so bad that the extended Schwartz family must live jammed up in the same apartment. Income is drained off for defense and old-age pensions. Diet consists of processed seaweed and sawdust—the only way to feed a population of twelve billion. Television pumps out the same old news items plus daytime serials that the Schwartzes have been watching for the past century.

The oldest Schwartz is Lou's grandfather, 172, who is king of the roost because he is oldest. Gramps possesses the only single room. He flaunts a last will and testament that he alters periodically to keep his brood in line. A tyrant, in short. As Lou tells his wife, "Gramps is never going to leave if somebody doesn't help him along a little." The rest of the story deals with "helping Gramps along a little," with an outcome that will make most readers glad to be living in our own time.

Such a fantasy warns that immortality may not be all it's cracked up to be. The fantasy also fleshes out the projections by pointing out the future miseries of a gerontocratic society if those projections are ignored.

268 *Author:* Walker, Alice
Title: "To Hell with Dying" (1967). In **In Love and Trouble: Stories of Black Women.** New York: HBJ, 1973
Genre: story
Commentary: This story describes a deep intergenerational affection, as well as its restorative powers. An old black widower, Mr. Sweet was "a diabetic and an alcoholic and a guitar player." The narrator tells of her girlhood, how she and the other children played with Mr. Sweet, who in spite of frequent drunkenness had a special charm for them. "We never felt anything of Mr. Sweet's age when we

played with him. We loved his wrinkles and would draw some on our brows to be like him."

By practical standards Mr. Sweet was something of a wreck. Barred by his blackness from becoming a doctor or lawyer or sailor as he once hoped, he turned to fishing, to haphazard farming, to brewing his own liquor, and to his guitar on which he played "all sorts of sweet, sad wonderful songs." Sometimes when he fell sick to death, the narrator's father would bring his children (especially the narrator, who was youngest) to Mr. Sweet's bed, saying, "To hell with dying. These children want Mr. Sweet!" Then the children would embrace the old man and actually revive him.

The narrator, now studying at the university, is called home once more to the deathbed of Mr. Sweet. This time he really dies, but not without recognizing her affectionate presence. The narrator now remembers him as "my first love."

In "The Welcome Table" (1973) from the same volume, a very old black woman totters to a white church on a winter Sunday morning and is expelled. "Singing in her head," she stands uncertainly on the church steps, when she sees Jesus striding down the highway toward her. When he says "Follow me," she does so joyfully. She is later found dead on the road. The story is remarkable for its description of white racism and its impact on the aged black, and for its showing the power of religious faith at the end of life.

269 *Author:* Welty, Eudora

Title: "A Visit of Charity" (1941). In **The Collected Stories of Eudora Welty.** San Diego, Calif.: HBJ, 1980

Genre: story

Commentary: A young girl has an unforgettable encounter with the contradictions and desperation of old age. Marian, 14, arrives one day at the Old Ladies' Home to gain "three points" as part of her Campfire Girls' service. She tells the nurse at the desk, "I have to pay a visit to some old lady." The nurse directs her to a room occupied by two old women.

Marian's visit is a traumatic one; nothing in her experience has prepared her for it. Instead of finding two passive, sweet old women who sit calmly in their rocking chairs and read their Bibles, Marian encounters two aged crones who argue heatedly, share some of their deepest secrets and fears, and probably confirm every negative stereotype the young girl has of old age. When Marian looks about the dark, cluttered interior of the room, she feels trapped, as if she were "caught in a robbers' cave, just before one was murdered."

Suddenly one of the women launches into a long diatribe against her roommate. She complains about being trapped with a "perfect stranger" who insists on talking so much that she feels she is losing her mind. Marian is drawn to this old woman and for the first time in her visit she ventures a question that is spontaneous and heart-felt: "How old are you?" When the old woman cries, "I won't tell!" Marian withdraws, escapes from the clutches of the other woman, and runs out of the Old Ladies' Home as if her very life depended upon it.

270   *Title:* "A Worn Path" (1941)
      Commentary: This story depicts an older person as caregiver, whose strength of character and purity of heart is more than a match for a sometimes hostile world (represented by forces in the natural and human environments). Phoenix Jackson, an old black woman, walks for miles along the Old Natchez Trace into Natchez to get more medicine for her young grandson, who had swallowed lye three years before. She overcomes all obstacles in her path to carry out her mission. She arrives in the city at Christmas time, and at the clinic the nurse recognizes her and gives her a bottle of the medicine to soothe the little boy's throat.

      The author portrays Phoenix Jackson in heroic terms as a woman of indomitable will and spirit. After encountering a young hunter on the trail, she notices that a nickel has fallen from his pocket. She uses her wiles to distract him so that she can pick up the money. Later, in the city, she directs a charitable gift of a few pennies by not-ing, "Five pennies is a nickel." With her second nickel in hand, she declares that she will buy her grandson a toy: "I'll march myself back where he is waiting, holding it straight up in this hand." In-spired by this new goal, she begins her journey back home.

271   *Author:* Wiser, William
      Title: "The Man Who Wrote Letters to Presidents." In **Ballads, Blues and Swan Songs.** New York: Atheneum, 1982
      Genre: story
      Commentary: The old person as lifelong loser is the center of this darkly comic episode. Paul Greer, 43, a hotel salad chef, is enjoying a drink at the bar when he is accosted by an old drifter who pro-

ceeds to bore and then frighten him with the account of his long guerilla warfare against the "system."

From the first World War to President Kennedy's time in the 1960s, this old fellow has written to United States presidents demanding benefits, warning against catastrophe, protesting job bias. To extort public attention to himself from time to time, he has swallowed objects ranging from glass to nail polish until his body is a surgery patchwork.

Though Paul's eyes glaze over at this recital, he begins to see how he too has been a loser or at best a small winner. His wartime marriage did not last beyond the honeymoon. His highest achievement was supervising the making of 700 lettuce-and-tomato salads for a single luncheon. His whole agenda for this evening had been to check his car for scratches and his tires for pressure. He leaves the old man in near panic, wondering which downfall was worse, the man's or his own.

The old man's monolog crackles with sarcastic wit about the "system." It evokes an elemental admiration, as if the reader might say, "That's the way for an old loser to go out!" Paul's response—his seeing himself in this wizened failure—suggests an advisability for middle age to look ahead at its own future.

272 *Author:* Yurick, Sol
   Title: "The Siege." In **Someone Just Like You.** New York: Harper, 1972
   Genre: story
   Commentary: This powerful story shows a strange corruption of humanitarian services to the destitute aged. Mrs. Diamond, an old slum welfare case, is besieged for two hours by Miller, the Relief Investigator, and Kalisher, a social worker. She will not let them see her fourth room, which they suspect may hold hidden assets that would disqualify her for aid.

Miller's rule is simple. Either the woman will allow the secret room to be checked or she will be cut off from relief. Losing patience, he becomes increasingly harsh. By contrast, Kalisher is gentle; he wants to win by persuasion and respect. As for Mrs. Diamond, the woman is ugly, underfed, long abandoned by husband and son, eking out her grimy life amid stench and disorder, so that Kalisher sees in her "all of the suffering, the poor, the sick, all the lonely, old, and deserted in the slums."

When the two men break her resistance at last, they enter the room in a kind of spiritual rape. They find nothing but her mad accumulation of rags, ribbons, swatches, and bolts of fabric. Yurick's story is appalling in its dissection of the old woman's diseased mind and the inhumane way in which a welfare system can treat people like her.

Plays

301 *Author:* Anderson, Robert
   Title: **I Never Sang for My Father**. New York: Dramatists Play Service, 1968
   Genre: play
   Commentary: In this two-act play, Anderson probes the fragile relationship between Gene Garrison, in his early forties, and his father, Tom. A central theme is stated by Gene in the beginning scene: "Death ends a life, but it does not end a relationship, which struggles on in the survivor's mind toward some final resolution, some clear meaning, which it perhaps never finds." The action of the play reveals that generations cannot always become reconciled to each other. Sometimes old people cannot adapt and change. Sometimes the bitter legacy of one's past is too great an obstacle to overcome.

Tom Garrison is a mean-spirited, selfish, angry old man who has never forgiven his own father for abandoning his family. Tom holds tight to a terrible memory of the time he threw his father off his mother's funeral coach because the old man was drunk. Abandoned by his father, Tom became the provider for his siblings, and he has always defined fatherhood as the source of food, shelter, and clothing—but not of love. Gene has always respected his father, feared him, stood in awe of him. But Gene has never loved his father, and he cannot forgive himself for not loving Tom. Gene holds fast to the "image" of the loving, sensitive father figure. But when he tries to apply that image to Tom, it crumbles in the face of his father's abrasive, self-centered behavior.

When Gene's mother dies suddenly, Gene and his sister, who comes home for the funeral, review Tom's influence on their lives and consider how best to resolve Tom's future. Tom will have nothing to do with their plans for live-in help. He assumes that Gene will visit him regularly, despite the fact that each time Gene tries to spend time with Tom both are left feeling irritable and unfulfilled. Gene is trapped. Nothing he can do will change the cycle of bitterness he has inherited from his father. Although he has always sought to love his father, his only recourse is to confront him. After an intense argument in the last scene of the play, Gene storms out of his father's house and never returns. His father dies a few years later. Gene's departure frees him from his father's domination, but nothing can liberate him from the need to have experienced a father's love.

302 *Author:* Beckett, Samuel

Title: **Krapp's Last Tape** (1958). In **Krapp's Last Tape and Other Dramatic Pieces**. New York: Grove, 1960

Genre: play

Commentary: Beckett's stark view of life—let alone of old age—is not for queasy stomachs. Those who have seen *Waiting for Godot* or *Endgame* know the grim pointlessness, the discontinuity, the pathos and stink, the doddering quest for meaning that make up Beckett's universe. Nonetheless, his characters are graced by their author's sardonic humor. In their darkness, they never quite give up but spin out fables of something better.

Krapp's Last Tape, a short drama with one actor, shows Krapp, a seedy old man on his birthday, as he listens to a tape recording of himself made on his thirty-ninth birthday. His boxes are full of such anniversary self-analyses. Here is "life review" to morbid excess, each review leading back to the same vices and narcissistic pretentions.

This older Krapp (the name hardly needs comment) is unkempt, untidy, cracked in voice, stiff in movement, wandering of mind, irascible of temper. He listens sarcastically to the younger Krapp, who reports having listened to a tape of a still younger Krapp with amusement at the youngest Krapp's resolutions to drink less, fornicate less, eat fewer bananas—all vices still practiced by the old Krapp. The younger Krapp, riding on what he thinks is the "crest of the wave" of his powers, alludes to a miraculous vision of his own meaning, an experience that set off a "fire" within him. But the older Krapp impatiently switches forward to a passage reporting the younger Krapp making love in a rowboat.

Again he switches off. He changes to a fresh tape and tries to make a new recording of the year just past; but his recent history is so trivial and even terminal that he throws away the new tape, puts back the old one, and listens once again to the love-making in the rowboat, which ends as the younger Krapp speaks of having lost any chance of happiness. The finished tape runs on in silence while the older Krapp sits motionless and staring.

303 *Author:* Coburn, D. L.
   Title: **The Gin Game**. New York: Drama Bo., 1978
   Genre: play
   Commentary: This tense two-act drama shows a spectacular way *not* to grow old. Two attractive residents of a home for the aged, man and woman, form a friendship centered on playing gin rummy. The friendship deteriorates as this strange and diabolical card game brings out the lifelong flaws that can surface during the stresses of old age.

   Fonsia Dorsey, between 65 and 70, has come to the Bentley Nursing and Convalescent Home allegedly because she did not want to turn over all her assets to the other institution she would have preferred. She meets Weller Martin, between 70 and 75, a retired businessman, a veteran of such homes. He introduces her to gin rummy, in the course of which they enjoy each other as witty, playful adults, a cut above the plaintive, disability-oriented, apathetic other inmates.

   By an odd subversion of the law of averages, Fonsia steadily wins at cards despite the other's self-proclaimed status as expert. Weller's constant defeat draws responses from him at ever-deeper levels, from patronizing compliment to wry resignation to indignant amazement to enraged profanity and finally to temper tantrum. Fonsia resists his demands to resume playing. She is frightened by him yet drawn by their mutual dependence. At length she succumbs to rage herself. Sadistically each prods into the other's genteel pretenses. Weller seemingly was an incompetent business man, deserted by family and partner, weakly blaming everything on bad luck. Fonsia, far from a charming lady, was a prudish and vindictive woman who evicted her husband, hated her son, and to spite him gave her home to the church. The play ends in climactic invective and imminent violence, with both characters drained of self-respect and hope for affection.

   The wit, blithe and later savage, is entertaining. The comments on the seedier side of nursing homes are instructive.

304 *Author:* Cooper, Susan, and Hume Cronyn
   Title: **Foxfire**. New York: French, 1983
   Genre: play
   Commentary: This two-act play, inspired by Eliot Wigginton's *Foxfire* series of oral histories, takes place in Rabun County, Georgia, and focuses on the experiences of three characters: Annie Nations, nearly 80, a widow, who lives alone on the farm "Stony Lonesome"

in the Blue Ridge Mountains; her husband, Hector; and her son, Dillard, 30, who is a country western music star. The play celebrates the bonds of love that exist between the old couple (they have been married for 55 years), identifies some of the enduring qualities of rural living, illustrates the importance of "place" for an old person, and demonstrates how the old renew their own lives when they respond to the needs of others.

An unusual dramatic technique helps readers understand the primary dramatic conflict in the play. The opening scene appears to begin with a simple conversation between Annie and Hector in the front yard. But after several scenes readers learn that Hector has been dead for five years. So Annie's "conversations" with Hector are in her imagination. Their conversations continue throughout the play. Annie holds onto the memory of Hector because she needs his "presence" to help her resolve her grief and to assist her in dealing with the essential question of the play: will she leave Stony Lonesome?

This issue is resolved when Annie's son, Dillard, who is giving a concert in town, appears suddenly. Dillard's wife has left him for another man, and he is faced with raising his two children alone. Although he wants Annie to help him raise the children, he doesn't force the issue. She comes to see that she is needed by her son and grandchildren, and she resolves Dillard's crisis by resolving her own—by deciding to leave Hector and the farm behind.

The characterization of the old couple is one of the strengths of the play. Hector is not perfect; in fact, he was an inflexible and intolerant father who drove three of his children away from home. Annie characterizes him in this way: "I ain't about t' put him on the same rung as th' Almighty, but I wouldn't be without him." Annie is portrayed as a no-nonsense woman who is strong-willed and devoted to her children.

305 *Author:* Gardner, Herb
Title: **I'm Not Rappaport**. New York: French, 1986
Genre: play
Commentary: Nat, eightyish, a quixotic hero and inspired liar, tries to cope with a heartless city, usually in support of downtrodden friends. In doing so, he assumes one fictitious identity after another, inventing so many sagas of himself that one hardly knows when to believe him. The scene is Central Park in New York.

An unwilling recipient of Nat's championship is his friend Midge, also eightyish, black, nearly blind, an incompetent janitor, a loser who wants only to stay inconspicuous in this brutal place. Nat assumes the identity of a tough union lawyer to stall off the tenants' representative charged with firing Midge. Nat becomes police officer Captain Danforth in the effort to rescue Midge from a thug "protector." Nat invents a love-child who will take him to Israel, away from the solicitous meddling of his daughter. He becomes Tony Donatto of the Mafia trying to scare off a drug dealer who threatens a young woman artist nearby.

Although these impersonations fail, the play remains an eloquent drama of courageous friendship in hard-driven old age. Nat's Act I manifesto on the old and their claims is memorable. The dialogue flashes with such lines as "I got a hip like a tea cup," "You ain't even *friendly* with the truth," and "You'll put me in a home for the forgettable." A secondary theme is the flowering, in old age, of Nat's lifelong temperament as a radical always fighting a lost cause.

The title is a line from a comic routine of mistaken identity, appropriate for a hero of chameleon personality.

306 *Author:* Harwood, Ronald
Title: **The Dresser**. New York: Grove, 1980
Genre: play
Commentary: The action follows one day in the life of an aging Shakesperean actor, known only as "Sir," and his dresser as they prepare for a performance of *King Lear*. The two are part of a ragged troupe of aging actors who perform several plays from Shakespeare each week, despite the perils of the Blitz. The time is January, 1942. The setting is a theater in the English provinces.

Sir is a pompous, raging, impotent, pathetic old man, living on the edge of desperation. He sees himself as a heroic figure who singlehandedly maintains the legacy of Shakespeare for the benefit of the unenlightened citizens of the Empire. What a magnificent contradiction! Sir is one part King Lear incarnate, one part Willy Loman, and one part Archie Rice, the consummate entertainer.

Insights into old age abound in the play. At one point Sir complains, "I want a tranquil senility. I'm a grown man. I don't want to go on painting my face night after night." At another point he is putting on the makeup for an old man, and he admits, "There was a time when I had to paint in all the lines. Now I merely deepen what is already there." As he becomes the character in his role as King Lear, he reminds us that the old have to endure untold hardships and pain. When he declares, "I am the storm!" his raging is the image of the defiant old hero who refuses to go "gentle" into that "good night."

His relationship with Norman, his dresser, is beset with complications. The two have been together for years, and Norman has a deep-seated admiration for the old man's native talent. At the same time, Norman is Sir's nursemaid, counselor, and confidant. So Norman is indispensable, and yet vulnerable. Without Sir, Norman is nothing. Unfortunately, Norman is left with nothing at the end of the play. After completing his performance of Lear, Sir dies of a heart attack, and Norman rages with grief at his sudden loss.

307   *Author:* Howe, Tina
      Title: **Painting Churches. In Three Plays by Tina Howe.** New York: Avon, 1984
      Genre: play
      Commentary: An artist, Mags Church, comes to paint a portrait of her old parents as they break up their Boston home of many years. In the process, all three Churches work through lifelong conflicts and end by seeing one another at his or her best.

      Mags' father, Gardner Church, is a distinguished poet, friend of poets such as Robert Frost and Ezra Pound. Though he still labors at a book of literary criticism, his powers have scattered, just like the books and papers in his disordered study. His attention span is momentary, his memory splintered, his emotions volatile and boyish. He is incontinent. Yet the old genius flashes through in unpredictable bursts of poetic recitation. Mags' mother, Fanny, of an old Boston family, is witty, excitable, and protective of her husband.

      In the compounded commotion of homecoming and moving, the three Churches enjoy each other—clowning, shouting, scolding, reminiscing, posing like ham actors. A serious theme comes to surface: Mags' lifelong feeling that her parents do not appreciate her creative gift. Another theme is the parents' feeling that Mags neglects them. Over all is the impending loss of talent, vitality, and a gracious life. The final scene, in which Mags' portrait stirs the old couple into an appreciative dance in the manner of the Impressionist painters, is a moving evocation of the grace that can descend on the final years of a life well lived.

308   *Author:* Jones, Preston
      Title: **The Oldest Living Graduate.** New York: Dramatists Play Service, 1976
      Genre: play
      Commentary: This bittersweet, thoroughly Texan drama presents the intergenerational struggle between a once-powerful parent and

his frustrated children. The time is 1962, the place Bradleyville, "a small, dead West Texas town."

Colonel J. C. Kincaid, a 75-year-old widower, is the "oldest living graduate" of Mirabeau Military Academy. A wheel-chair survivor of the first World War, he is besieged by his son Floyd to surrender claim to the Genet farm, an old family holding that Floyd and a partner want to convert into a posh lakeside development. Their conflict runs deep. The Colonel had once loved the daughter on that farm, and though he lost her, he still clings to his magic times there. For Floyd and his wife, the farm offers a way out of their stagnation in this dead town.

Toward the climax, Floyd reveals that he has secretly declared his father incompetent, thus forcing the turnover of the Genet farm. The Colonel is brought in after suffering a serious stroke, probably terminal. The son gives up his ambition for the land just as the old Colonel, accepting the loss of life and memories, surrenders the land. His curtain summary of the life he leaves is moving.

These serious currents run under much lively comedy. The Colonel is a master of fulminating invective. Maureen, his acid-witted daughter-in-law, uses an enjoyably sharp tongue. One episode involves a hilarious parody of old southern military-school culture.

The Oldest Living Graduate is third of *A Texas Trilogy*, which deals with related characters in the same community.

309 *Author:* McEnroe, Robert E.
Title: **The Silver Whistle.** New York: Dramatists Play Service, 1949
Genre: play
Commentary: The scene is a drab, depressed old people's home operated by a penurious church. A new inmate arrives—Oliver Erwenter, whose strangely youthful spirit and appearance suggest that he is something of a sprite, a Pan figure, a Pied Piper. His mission, it seems, is to lead these aging souls back into the country of youth. The play itself, though a fantasy, raises a serious challenge about how far one must surrender to the trials of old age and how far to retain a spirit of adventure.

Bit by bit, Erwenter wins the inmates to a more exciting view of themselves. Mr. Beebe, a gentle white-haired man whose main hope at the outset was for a beautiful funeral, is brought to believe in his romantic stirrings toward the coquettish Mrs. Sampler. Mrs. Harmer, the resident curmudgeon, at last joins the common project of throwing a bazaar to raise funds. Even young Miss Tripp, the careworn superintendent, feels the attraction of this stranger; and so does the Reverend Watson, her stuffy fiancé. By the play's end, this sad little community has found rejuvenation and even joy.

The secret of Erwenter's magic is partly confidence game: bluffs and tall tales that stimulate his audience. Partly he feels a genuine zeal for the wandering, daring life, as often brought out in his visionary speeches. Actually Erwenter is a young man in his forties, conducting in this visit a personal experiment to find "if there is any point in living to be seventy-seven." His answer is affirmative. The fact that he *is* young, not old, introduces an intergenerational theme: the role that younger persons can play in improving the morale of the old.

The title of the play comes from this jingle: "The old dog crawled away to die and hid amid the thistle. / Then joy and youth came back to him on the note of a Silver Whistle."

310 *Author:* Miller, Arthur
Title: **Death of a Salesman**. New York: Viking, 1949
Genre: play
Commentary: This intense drama has become virtually the American classic on aging as an ordeal forcing together the lies and truths of the whole life.

Willy Loman, aged 63, has spent 36 years as the New England salesman of his New York company. He has lived by the American success dream that insists that "being well liked" is the secret, that jokes and glad-handing together with some ruthlessness will see one to the top. He has passed this ethic on to his two sons, Biff and Happy, with whom as boys he once enjoyed close comradeship—polishing the car, fixing the yard, playing sports. Willy worships Biff, the elder son, a fine athlete whom Willy spurs on to win games even at the cost of cheating at studies. Biff's stealing athletic equipment he sees as high-spirited pranks. One symbol of this hard-punching quick success ethic is Willy's older brother Ben, who appears in fantasy to utter his battle song: "When I was seventeen, I walked into the jungle, and when I was twenty-one I walked out. And by God I was rich."

The dark truth of Willy's life is that he never rose far as salesman. He has lied about his failures and his borrowing from a neighbor. Under his hearty manner he has felt shy and lonely and "temporary" about himself, needing to womanize on the road. His favorite son, Biff, left high school without finishing and never justified his father's worship of him as a triumphant Adonis. On Biff's return from itinerant farm work, the two quarrel savagely. Willy is now too exhausted and anxious to stay on the road. He is denied the secure desk job he has hoped for and instead is heartlessly fired as useless.

Behind these clashing scenarios, Willy has always been haunted by a dim dream of a simpler, wholesome life in the open, where a man could be himself, could raise vegetables and chickens, could enjoy his family.

Past and present rush concurrently through Willy's mind, which is the main stage of action. Thus Willy's conflicting life-visions flash one against the other in compelling dramatization of his breaking mind. In this last day of life, after a brief resurrection of optimism, Willy has his final quarrel with Biff over its real cause: Biff's traumatic discovery, at the end of high school, of his father's infidelity. This welling-up of fundamental grief somehow purges the relationship and allows the old father-son love to come through once more. Willy is prepared for his climactic sacrifice for Biff, a suicidal car crash that will yield a large insurance pay-off. A brief requiem scene at the cemetery summarizes some of the conflicts in Willy's life.

311 *Author:* Shakespeare
   Title: **King Lear** (1606)
   Genre: play
   Commentary: This great tragedy illuminates the ordeals and triumphs of old age with a breadth and grandeur that make it the all-time masterpiece on aging. Shakespeare's language, especially in the "mad" scenes, is sometimes difficult, but a well-annotated edition (of which there are many) should see the serious reader through.

Old King Lear, a once-powerful leader in the mythical depths of history, "retires" from his throne, dividing his kingdom among his three daughters, Goneril, Regan, and Cordelia. In return, this foolish monarch bargains with them to allot the largest share to the daughter who loves him most. The oldest two have no trouble feeding the old man the loving speeches he wants to hear. Cordelia is too proud to sell herself in this manner and is instantly disinherited by her enraged father. Lear goes ahead with his self-serving scenario. In return for settling his kingdom upon Goneril and Regan, he directs them to take turns hosting him and his retinue of a hundred knights. He further expects them to go on treating him with all the honor due royalty.

Any modern-day retiree who has expected to continue enjoying all the prestige and attention received in the prime of life can anticipate what happens to Lear. He is quickly discounted. Goneril and

Regan, supposing that he will become more unpredictable and arbitrary with advancing age, collude to strip him of the power he has retained. Lear finds himself first mistreated in the home of Goneril, then entirely impoverished by both daughters. The scene in which the old father protests this abuse of age and then breaks into tears (Act II, Scene 4) is one of the strongest in the play. Its argument easily translates into contemporary terms.

Maddened by finding that the world he lives in is much crueler than he ever supposed in his days of comfort, Lear wanders the countryside through a raging storm. He rages against universal injustice, calls for divine punishment of humanity, and in a touching passage recognizes how much he shares with the underprivileged of the world:

> Poor naked wretches, wheresoe'er you are,
> That bide the pelting of this pitiless storm,
> How shall your houseless heads and unfed sides,
> Your looped and windowed raggedness, defend you
> From seasons such as these? Oh, I have ta'en
> Too little care of this! [Act III, Scene 4]

The wrecked old king, who is finally rescued by the invading army of his exiled daughter Cordelia, has learned his own weakness; he has learned compassion; he has learned to recognize the true love of his faithful child. Although the two are destroyed by the forces of the evil sisters, their discovery of love and true worth mounts above the general holocaust of war and multiplied treachery.

Shakespeare's plays are above all meant to be *acted*. Readers may well try reading critical scenes aloud (with or without action). After studying the text, they may deepen their enjoyment by seeing an actual performance or videotape of the play.

312 *Author:* Thompson, Ernest
Title: **On Golden Pond**. New York: Dodd, 1979
Genre: play
Commentary: An affectionate old couple spend perhaps their last season at the old family summer home on Golden Pond in Maine. They suffer the anxieties of physical decline. They work out a lifelong tension with their adult daughter. They enjoy coming to know a lively boy in place of the grandchildren they never had. They taste once more the simple pleasures and friendship they have always treasured here. Finally, they experience, beneath the banter and fencing, the real depth of their love.

Norman Thayer, 79, a retired professor, and his younger wife, Ethel, open the new season on Golden Pond. Described in the stage directions as "boyish and peppery," Norman is contentious with others, both playfully and sadistically. His manner conceals a fear of death, a distress over his failures of memory, and a nervousness about his fortyish daughter Chelsea. When Chelsea arrives for his eightieth birthday, she is once more the little fat girl being picked on by her dad. Parent and child use this one great chance to reconcile. Bill Ray, 13-year-old son of her future husband, forms a lovely friendship with the old man that allows Norman's younger self to make an encore appearance. Throughout, Norman's wife shows the courageous wit and understanding to help him toward their day of serene farewell to Golden Pond.

313   *Author:* Uhry, Alfred
    Title: **Driving Miss Daisy**. New York: Lexington, 1988
    Genre: play
    Commentary: Daisy Werthan, seventyish, a well-to-do hard-willed Jewish widow, gradually mellows under her own increasing help-lessness and sensitive management by others.

She has been having so many auto accidents that her son, Boolie, insists that she take a chauffeur, whom he hires: a black man, Hoke Coleburn, fiftyish. The conflict between this aged autocrat and her servant makes the play. Daisy resents being looked after. She vehemently rejects Hoke's diplomatic advances, not even allowing him to drive for the first week of his employment. Bit by bit, his engaging and subtle tact wins her to tolerate his service and then, as the years pass, to depend on it. Hoke, for his part, has a simple dignity that can assert itself when Daisy's arrogance goes too far.

Daisy's rejection of Hoke reaches a dramatic point when the synagogue is bombed, a crushing cruelty. When Hoke tries to tell how his own people have suffered lynching, she shrills at him, "Don't talk to me!" Later, she softens enough to want to attend a dinner in honor of the great black leader, Martin Luther King, Jr. Her son Boolie refuses to go with her; as a Jewish businessman cautiously thriving in the gentile culture of Atlanta, he declines the risk. Instead he dares Daisy to invite Hoke. When Hoke drives her to the church, she stammers out a hint that he would be welcome. He proudly refuses such a grudging invitation.

So this long conflict reaches a kind of balance. As Daisy passes ninety, she has a stroke and becomes disoriented. When Hoke rallies to help, she says touchingly, "You're my best friend." At the end

Hoke visits her in a nursing home and feeds her as she mumbles contentedly. At this basic level, the friendship is complete. A difficult aging has ended in harmony.

314 *Author:* Wilder, Thornton
Title: **The Long Christmas Dinner**. New York: French, 1931
Genre: play
Commentary: Ninety years in the life of the Bayard family are condensed into one long Christmas dinner in this one-act celebration of the life cycle. As parents and relatives age, they put on wigs of white hair and eventually move out through the dark portal that denotes death. Children enter through the flowery portal that denotes life, then mature, and eventually follow their forebears.

All the while, the dinner conversation flows on. Old Mother Bayard recounts crossing the Mississippi River and seeing Indians. Later the Bayards speak of a growing town and business, of World War I, and of the urbanization that surrounds the old home. Finally, the stage empties as the last widow departs to live with her children in a new family center where the cycle presumably will continue.

In all this, Wilder shows the wonderful range of experience that makes up a family. There are the repeated rituals ("A glass of wine with you, sir") and repeated commonplaces ("Every least twig is wrapped around with ice; you almost never see that"). There is joy over births, fear of oncoming death, remorse over lost chances to value the dead, myths of the days long gone by. The rebellion of the young enters in, as well as war, decay, and final scattering to resume elsewhere.

The Long Christmas Dinner affirms the life that, however quickly it streams along, conveys an enduring worth. The play is a thank offering, not for old age only, but for the whole of life and its coming and growing and passing. It illuminates aging by showing its optimum context in a continuum of family achievement, affection, appreciation, memory.

Poems

401 *Author:* Auden, W. H.
Title: "Old People's Home" (1970). In **W. H. Auden: Collected Poems**. Ed. by Edward Mendelson. New York: Random, 1976
Commentary: Riding the subway on the way to a half-hour visit with an old friend who resides in a nursing home, the poet muses about the status of the old people who are residents of the home. He categorizes them as the "elite" (those who are ambulatory and mentally sound), "those on wheels" (who suffer various therapies and forced interactions with other residents), the "loners" (who suffer from irreversible mental and physical disabilities), and the "terminally incompetent" (who are as stolid and unknowing as plants). These categories reflect the poet's anger and frustration at what old age may offer the individual.

He concludes that in previous generations the role for the old was well defined. Their wisdom and experience were valued, and they were an integral part of families: "Then a child, / in dismay with Mamma, could refuge with Gran / to be revalued and told a story." Auden understands that this "generation / is the first to fade like this, not at home but assigned / to a numbered frequent ward, stowed out of conscience / as unpopular luggage." At the end of the poem, he recalls the old woman he will be visiting. He realizes that this visit is less a "presumptive joy" than "a good work" on his part, and he feels the loss that this attitude expresses. He wonders if it is wrong to hope for an early death for this old woman.

402 *Title:* "Doggerel by a Senior Citizen" (1969)
Genre: poem
Commentary: The fourteen stanzas of this poem, written in rhyming couplets, provide a whimsical comparison of the modern world to the "good old days" of Edwardian England. The narrator of the poem decries the changes wrought by progress, changes in religious practice, new sexual attitudes, greater permissiveness in educational philosophies, and the decline of the English language. Auden, who was 62 when he wrote the poem, perhaps identifies with the narra-

tor's complaint that the modern world has become overly complicated and devoid of a moral center.

He insists, however, that one thing has not changed:

> But Love, at least, is not a state
> Either *en vogue* or out-of-date,
> And I've true friends, I will allow,
> To talk and eat with here and now.

He vows to carry on by engaging life in the present rather than
simply yearning for times that are past. Auden makes playful use of
"doggerel" verse, poetry that is usually considered trivial and me-
chanical in rhyme and rhythm.

403 *Author:* Brooks, Gwendolyn
   Title: "Jessie Mitchell's Mother" (1960). In **The World of Gwendo-
      lyn Brooks**. New York: Harper, 1971
   Genre: poem
   Commentary: This brief poem (just over one page) conveys a stark
   vision of a desolate old woman in poverty, clinging to former joys
   while the adult daughter sees in her mother only the moribund
   wreckage.
      A black daughter visits her mother's bedroom "to wash the bal-
   looning body" of a woman with "brains of jelly, sweet, quiver-soft,
   irrelevant." The daughter reflects: "Only a habit would cry if she
   should die."
      The old mother in turn looks at her daughter. She sees the young
   straight body and thinks of all the hardships that bend and destroy
   poor women. One spiteful consolation is her memory of her own
   youthful loveliness, so much finer. She ends with reviving the
   "dried-up triumphs" of her "exquisite yellow youth."

404 *Author:* Ciardi, John
   Title: "Obit." In **Echoes: Poems Left Behind by John Ciardi**. Fayette-
      ville: Univ. of Arkansas Pr., 1989
   Genre: poem
   Commentary: The consequences of a lifetime of vain and fruitless
   striving is recounted in this "obituary." Here is someone who was always "looking for something to do." Unfortunately, the man never is
   able to attach meaning to his accomplishments. Although what he
   did for a living is not indicated, one may infer that he spent his pre-
   retirement years searching for some purpose, some reason for being,
   and not finding it. After retirement he continues his search. At the

age of 69 he starts a new business and makes a fortune in five years. Then he sells the business, starts collecting stamps, becomes bored, and dies. That's his story. But the poet adds a close to *this* obituary that rings with irony when one considers all that this man appeared to accomplish. After the years of searching, the man finds only one truth: "it doesn't matter how much you get through / day after day when there is nothing to do."

405   *Title:* "Matins"
Commentary: This angry poem reflects on how little human life is sometimes valued, especially the life of anonymous street people who are old. The poet responds to a brief story in the newspaper about a woman, "too tattered-old to notice," who was found frozen to death on a park bench. When he considers how much money is spent on processing the dead body, he wonders if that money could have been better spent on making her life more bearable.

406   *Title:* "December 13, 1979"
Commentary: An old man's observation of three squirrels playing outside on a winter day leads to a subtle comparison between the two worlds of youth and old age. Bemused by the squirrel's frenetic activity, the poet concludes that the squirrels feel secure in their play because they know that the man's old dog is no threat to them. His dog, "old and stiff, his monster slacked," is in no condition to chase squirrels.

Two other poems provide glimpses of old age. "The Aging Lovers" is a six-line poem that celebrates the agelessness of human love and passion. The poet reflects on the mutual desire felt by "two old crocks of habit." "An Old Man Confesses" is a jeremiad spoken by a man who admits that he is "bored by death" and disgusted at the evidence of physical decline he sees in his body.

407   *Author:* Eberhart, Richard
Title: "Half-Bent Man" (1958). In **Collected Poems 1930–1976**. New York: Oxford Univ. Pr., 1976
Genre: poem
Commentary: The "profound, heavy purpose" in the humble drudgeries of old age is seen by the poet in the haunting sight of an old trash-picker on a university campus. Half-bent to earth, the man trudges about, spearing stray papers, picking up rags, "ridding

the earth of detail and debris." In him is seen "a true condition" despite the towers, books, ideas, and professors that mingle in the world beyond him. He remains "a true condition," a parable in humility, to remind one that even the most talented of human beings are little more than "half-bent" creatures, picking "what gems and scraps there are from magnificence."

408   *Title:* "Hardy Perennial" (1972)
Commentary: The poet desires in old age to love every detail of the living. The theme of the poem is twice voiced as a kind of refrain: "In youth we dream of death, / In age we dream of life." Youth is described in the first half of the poem as reckless of risk, ready to test death by defying it. Age is described in the second half as aware of "death's savagery. . . / Each day nipping at my generation" and negating the venturesome drive of youth. In its place the aged speaker would "give love to every being alive, . . . / Discovering subtleties and profundities in / Any slightest gesture, or delicate glance."

Three other poems focus on aging. "The Tobacconist of Eighth Street" (1949) describes a talkative, fearful old tobacconist overtaken by ruin. In the old man's disappearance the speaker, in terror, sees the mortality that links them both. In "An Old Fashioned American Business Man," the old businessman speaks of the cold-blooded, ruthless career he followed even into his eighties, only to say now, "I wish for the love I did not give." "Autumnal" is a compact, even cryptic assertion by the speaker that in the final season of life, the world is still full of harvest.

409   *Author:* Emerson, Ralph Waldo
    Title: "Terminus" (1867). In **Poems of Ralph Waldo Emerson.**
    Selected by J. Donald Adams. New York: Crowell, 1965
  Genre: poem
  Commentary: One of the last poems of the great New England moralist, "Terminus" was written when Emerson was 63, perhaps aware of his own diminishing powers. Its opening lines convey the whole theme: "It is time to be old, / To take in sail." Then, in a series of brief vivid metaphors, the speaker counsels himself to reduce his ambitions, to "wisely accept the terms" of oncoming old age, but by no means to lie idle. For a little while, one can "still plan and smile." One can still select one's agenda instead of trying to do everything. Even though originality may dry up, one can still "mature the unfallen fruit" by finishing up those projects already con-

ceived. One must accept the defects in one's heredity that shorten one's energies. Above all, one can still rest without fear in a lifelong religious faith that will bring all souls home to port.

410 *Author:* Frost, Robert
Title: "The Death of the Hired Man" (1914). **In The Poetry of Robert Frost**. Ed. by Edward Connery Lathem. New York: Holt, 1969
Genre: poem
Commentary: This poem dramatizes the plight of the homeless aged, without money, without negotiable skills, without family, without any claim based on past achievement. The hired man of the title is old Silas, a worn-out farm laborer who has come "home" to the only couple to have given him a sense of stability.

The poem is narrated as a dialogue between the couple, Mary and Warren, as they debate what to do about the old man collapsed in the next room. When Mary asks her husband to "be kind," he flares up, reciting his many kindnesses to a hired man who always left when most needed, simply to earn a little money besides the keep he received from Warren. "I'll not have the fellow back. I told him so last haying, didn't I? If he left then, I said, that ended it."

But Silas *is* back, under the transparent pretext of coming to ditch the meadow. Mary goes on to describe how the old man is reminiscing confusedly, about haying here years ago with a college boy. The two had quarreled enjoyably about book knowledge versus folk knowledge; now Silas would like one more chance to set the lad straight. The fact is that Silas has come home to die. When Warren asks what she could mean by "home," Mary returns the memorable answer:

Home is the place where, when you have to go there,
They have to take you in.

Where else can this old drifter go? He has a wealthy brother whom he is too proud to approach. Other than that, Silas is a lifetime loser, never a criminal but never "quite as good as anybody." Once more admonished by his wife to be gentle, Warren goes to check on the old man. He comes back to report that Silas is dead.

Frost's famous short poem, "Stopping by Woods on a Snowy Evening" (1923), does not explicitly treat aging, but it has often been read as expressing a desire for the serenity of death, countered by the recognition that "I have promises to keep, / And miles to go before I sleep." Such promises presumably hold true into the late years. Another short poem, "Provide, Provide" (1936), serves up a cynical pill: aging people are foolish if they count on past attractiveness to comfort them in their later years.

411 *Author:* Graves, Robert
 Title: "The Great-Grandmother" (1938). In **Collected Poems 1966 by Robert Graves.** Garden City, N.Y.: Doubleday, 1966
 Genre: poem
 Commentary: A lifelong secret rebellion against the role of an aristocratic lady emerges in the confession of the great-grandmother, "that aged woman with the bass voice." The speaker is addressing the woman's great-grandchildren. He tells them how the woman lived a lie to children and grandchildren, and how at long last she is ready to confess to these distant descendants. She has disliked the "music, sighs, and roses" forced on her as a woman. She has disliked the "ailing poor" whom she was expected, as a privileged lady, to care for. A rather hard woman at heart, she really valued money, clean brass and linen, and, above all, solitude. Still, out of pride she acted the role of gracious lady until now, when "she has outlasted all man-uses." She has contentment at last and wisdom. She is worth listening to. (The poem bears comparison with Victoria Sackville-West's novel, *All Passion Spent*; see number 123.)

412 *Title:* "Nightmare of Senility" (1965). In **Poems 1970–1972 by Robert Graves.** Garden City, N.Y.: Doubleday, 1973
 Commentary: Written when Graves was 70, this chilling poem expresses the contrast between the youthful heart of the aged speaker and the wasted appearance of his mate. Thus it voices a common dismay among older people who continue to think and feel as lovers though their physical attractiveness seems ravaged. What the speaker asks for is an end to the hypocrisy by which the woman still pretends to a romantic fascination and the man pretends to accept it. As he sees it, "I watch you shrinking to a wrinkled hag, / Your kisses grow repulsive, your feet shuffle / And drag. Now I forget your name and forget mine. . . ." The poem is a nightmare as its title says, but an honest nightmare needing to be confronted.

Briefer poems on themes of aging (all from *Collected Poems 1966*): "The Face in the Mirror" (1958) is a humorous contemplation of the speaker's aged face in the mirror, as he wonders that he is still ready for romance. In "A Last Poem" (1964) the poet wonders when he can ever retire from his art. "The Septuagenarian" (1964) is a warning that the aged listener can no longer count on the indulgences given to youthful boasting; boasting has now become evidence of senility.

413 *Author:* Hardy, Thomas
    Title: "An Ancient to Ancients" (1922). In **The Complete Poems of Thomas Hardy**. Ed. by James Gibson. New York: Macmillan, 1978
    Genre: poem
    Commentary: The passing of one's own aging generation is elegized by the speaker, who is addressing his comrades ("Gentlemen"). Their old favorite dance halls are now in ruins. These gentlemen are now forgotten on the shores of the waters they once sailed and rowed on. Each year their ranks are thinned, in reminder that they will never again enjoy youth and romance. Their old dance-steps, their favorite operas, painters, novelists, and poets have faded with the past.

    Although their generation is hard-pressed by the younger and is soon to leave the scene, the speaker reminds them of ancient generations who, though approaching the end, "burnt brightlier." Such were Sophocles, Plato, Homer, and others.

    Turning at last to the rising generation, "red-lipped and smooth-browed," the speaker leaves them with the encouragement that they will find and enjoy much that his own generation has missed. So he bids farewell.

414 *Title:* "I Look into My Face" (1898)
    Commentary: In this brief but eloquent poem, the aging speaker views his wasting face in the mirror and feels the troubling force of young love in an aged body.

    "Would to God," he laments, that his heart had shrunk like his face. Then, not caring, he could endure the indifference of others. The punishing irony of age is that he must lose his physical attractiveness while still being shaken by desire.

    Thomas Hardy was a prolific late Victorian poet (and novelist) whose verses read clearly and carry a sense of drama, of people speaking or thinking in imagined situations. Two other poems that touch on themes of aging are "Former Beauties" (1909), lamenting the transformation of the beautiful women of one's youth into middle-aged market-dames, and "The Orphaned Old Maid"

(1909), in which an aging woman tells of having spent her life tending to a father now dead.

415 *Author:* Jacobsen, Rolf
      Title: "Old Age." In **Twenty Poems**. Trans. by Robert Bly. Madison,
            Minn.: Seventies Pr., 1977
      Genre: poem
      Commentary: Jacobsen, a Danish poet, portrays old age as a time
of integration, and he views the old with admiration and respect. In
"Old Age" the poet suggests that the old lead lives that are fragile
and yet resilient. He uses analogies to convey the variety of tasks
and roles that all people face in a long life. He compares the old to
"fishermen along big rivers" and to "convalescents whose feet still
are not very sturdy under them." In both cases the old possess almost mystical characteristics; they are "motionless as a stone" and
"they have something in their eyes."
      The end of life leads to resolution and affirmation. The old
"gradually become themselves once more." They "gradually break
up / like smoke, no one notices it, they are gone / into sleep / and
light." The last word, "light," offers a marked contrast to the expected "darkness" or "death." It conveys a positive, hopeful tone.
The analogy to "smoke" suggests that the old possess an evanescent
quality. They are most themselves when they appear to be least substantial. Like the sages in the Taoist philosophical tradition, they accomplish everything by doing nothing.

416 *Title:* "The Old Women"
      Commentary: The poet meditates on the transitory nature of life
and invites readers to reevaluate their attitudes toward old women.
He contrasts the lives of young women, whose "feet moved so fast,"
with the lives of "old women with narrow hands [who] climb up
stairs slowly." These old women seem to have outlived their generation and now live solitary lives. "No one understands their expressions any more." The poet suggests that these old women are worthy
of respect and even admiration. The poet implores readers to "Bow
clearly to them and greet them with respect / because they still carry
everything with them, like a fragrance. . . ."

      Another Jacobsen poem, "Memories of Horses," characterizes the
old as special people because "they take with them their secret language . . . all the signs the heart gathers up in the lean year."

417 *Author:* Jarrell, Randall
  Title: "The Face" (1955). In **Randall Jarrell: The Complete Poems.**
    New York: Farrar, 1969
  Genre: poem
  Commentary: The agony of seeing one's youth and beauty pass away is expressed by an aristocratic old lady as she stares into her mirror. "Not good any more, not beautiful—not even young. This isn't mine," she says. She wonders where the old pictures are that showed her loveliness.

  When people tell her, as people often tell the aged, "You haven't changed," she wants to reply with quiet bitterness, "You haven't looked." The old Marschallin (field marshal's wife) goes on to lament, as the aging so often do: "I'm not like this. I'm the same as always inside." But she knows that even that isn't so. She ends, once more at the mirror: "If just living can do this, living is more dangerous than anything. It's terrible to be alive."

  This 27-line poem is simple and poignant. Jarrell borrowed its situation from Strauss's opera, *Der Rosencavalier* in which "the old woman, the old Marschallin," speaks those words of herself as she looks into the glass.

418 *Title:* "Aging" (1960)
  Commentary: The aging speaker bemoans the ever-quickening passing of the hours, which stream away too fast for finding one's true self. What is wanted is a child's Sunday afternoon, a study hour when outside time one could "make a life." This short poem (16 lines) expresses the desire, often stronger as the days grow fewer, to recover or discover one's essential identity.

  Two other poems center on aging. "A Well-to-Do Invalid" (1965) comments on the caretakers of the old, whose self-sacrifice may be adulterated with possessiveness and may in the end be undervalued. "Money" (1955) is the amusing monologue of a peppery old millionaire who uses philanthropy as a final means of enjoying his power.

419 *Author:* Joseph, Jenny
  Title: "Warning." In **When I Am an Old Woman I Shall Wear Purple: An Anthology of Short Stories and Poetry.** Ed. by Sandra Martz, Manhattan Beach, Calif.: Papier-Maché Pr., 1987.
  Genre: poem
  Commentary: The first line of this poem is the title of the anthology in which it appears, a collection of works about and mainly by

women. The line announces the theme of the poem: old age is to be
a time of glorious self-indulgence. Besides purple, the speaker will
wear "a red hat which doesn't suit me." Her pension will go to
"brandy and summer gloves." She will express herself recklessly, at
risk of becoming a public nuisance:

> I shall sit down on the pavement when I am tired
> And gobble up samples in shops and press alarm bells
> And run my stick along the public railings
> And make up for the sobriety of my youth.

She will let herself go in diet, in "terrible shirts," in hoarding
whatever trifles she pleases.

However, at present the speaker and her middle-aged generation
must live proper, disciplined lives. "We must. . . pay our rent and
not swear in the street / And set a good example for the children."
Still, "Maybe I ought to practice a little now" so that people won't
be shocked "When suddenly I am old, and start to wear purple."

The poem is a cheerful warning to live more on impulse, to enjoy
one's own tastes, to enter old age as a time for individual personal
expansion.

420 *Author:* Larkin, Philip
     Title: "The Old Fools" (1973). In **Collected Poems**. Ed. by Anthony
          Thwaite. New York: Farrar, 1989
     Genre: poem
     Commentary: The narrator asks a series of blunt questions about
     the desperate existence of "the old fools," those old people who end
     their lives drooling, "crippled," incontinent, and senile. The poet
     begins by asking, "What do they think has happened, the old fools,
     / To make them like this?" Of course, no answer is forthcoming.
     The narrator's tone implies his extreme bitterness and anger at the
     processes of aging that lead to serious physical and psychological
     decline. The images of old age are dark and foreboding: "And these
     are the first signs: / Not knowing how, not hearing who, the power
     / Of choosing gone." After summarizing such symptoms of decline,
     the narrator is aghast that these old people don't share his outrage:
     "Why aren't they screaming?"

     The poet concludes that these old people don't evaluate their for-
     lorn existence. Instead, they reside in a private world that is removed
     from the experiences of others:

> Perhaps being old is having lighted rooms
> Inside your head, and people in them, acting.

People you know, yet can't quite name; each looms
Like a deep loss restored, from known doors turning, ...

In this interior world the old who seem out of touch with the "here and now" exist securely in a world where "all happened once." From the narrator's perspective this world offers little consolation for what has been lost; he can only ask more unanswered questions: "Can they never tell / What is dragging them back, and how it will end? Not at / night? / Not when the strangers come?"

The narrator ends with a bitter reference to this aspect of old age as a "hideous inverted childhood." He returns to the questions he posed earlier with a final ironic comment: "Well / We shall find out."

Larkin's bleak view of old age—one that demands honest recognition—shows in several briefer poems. "Love Songs in Age" (1957) describes a widow who stumbles upon the old song sheets of her youth and weeps over the unfulfilled promise these songs had held forth. In "Long Last" (1963) a senile old woman is seen in her confusion after the death of her younger sister. "Heads in the Women's Ward" (1972) takes a stark view of mindless geriatric patients in their beds. A milder but cautionary portrait is that of "Schoolmaster" (1940), about a man who chose teaching for its decorous security and continued such a lifelong retreat from real living that he finally "dissolved" in old age "like sugar in a cup of tea."

One kinder piece is the short "New Eyes Each Year" (1979), in which Larkin, himself a librarian, sees that in books, "Youth and age / Like ink and page / In this house join, / Minting new coin."

421 *Author:* Lawrence, D. H.
   Title: "Shadows." In **The Complete Poems of D. H. Lawrence.** Ed. by Vivian de Sola Pinto and Warren Roberts. New York: Viking, 1971
   Genre: poem
   Commentary: This is one of several Lawrence poems that express faith in the afterlife. The speaker begins with the analogy of sleep: how its oblivion refreshes so that he can "wake like a new-opened flower . . . dipped again in God, and new-created." Then he thinks of the passing weeks: how the moon and his spirit may darken but not his confidence that "I am walking still / with God, we are close together now the moon's in shadow."

The speaker goes on to consider the whole range of his possible extinctions: from obscurity of mind to pain with bodily disintegration. In all, he sees the shaping hand of "the unknown God" who can bring "odd, wintry flowers upon the withered stem. . .new blossoms of me." As death nears, the speaker will still know that this God "is breaking me down to his own oblivion / to send me forth on a new morning, a new man."

Two other poems that convey a similar assurance are "Gladness of Death" and "The Ship of Death."

Four short poems describe the stubborn, cantankerous, self-willed old age of those who have resisted true life, as well as the resentment, envy, and vampiric possessiveness they feel toward the young: "Old People," "The Grudge of the Old," "Old Men," and "Death." A contrasting poem, "Beautiful Old Age," envisions age as it might come at the end of a good life: "It ought to be lovely to be old / to be full of the peace that comes of experience / and wrinkled ripe fulfillment."

422 *Author:* MacLeish, Archibald
  Title: "The Wild Old Wicked Man" (1968). In **Archibald MacLeish: Collected Poems 1917–1982**. Boston: Houghton, 1985
  Genre: poem
  Commentary: Like the aged speaker troubled with "throbbings of noontide" in Thomas Hardy's poem, "I Look into My Glass," the speaker wonders how it is that he can be "too old for love and still to love!" All men, he thinks, are like aging Adams who still strut their pretense of sexuality. He likens this endless stirring of passion to the love cry of the wood dove in the darkening thorn grove. He likens it to evenings when all falls quiet but still "some passion in the sea beats on and on."

  Why this sexual restlessness? Does it express the longing for still one more proof of youth and vigor? Or does it spring from an intuition that some vital impulse in humanity is inextinguishable? And is the wicked old man a victor because he pursues this impulse?

  The speaker alludes early to the poet W. B. Yeats, who felt a similar question. The poem bears comparison to Yeats' poem of the same title (see number 446).

In brief poems, MacLeish often reflected on aging, with varied moods and insights, as in the following: "Definitions of Old Age"

(1985) is a dry look into the decline of old age when "even your own thoughts sound wrong to you, something some old idiot has misquoted." "The Old Gray Couple" (1973) is an affectionate, bantering dialogue between lovers after their fiftieth anniversary, who know that "love, like light, grows dearer toward the dark." "Unfinished History" (1933) expresses the fear of younger lovers that they must some day shiver in the ashes of passion. "With Age Wisdom" (1962) draws a comic contrast between the cynicism of the speaker at age 20 and, at age 60, his joyous wonder at life. "[Old Age]" (1985) humorously compares old age to living in a town that has changed out of recognition because of being torn up for new highways.

423 *Author:* Merwin, W. S.
   Title: "Grandfather in the Old Men's Home" (1960). In **Selected Poems**. New York: Atheneum, 1988
   Genre: poem
   Commentary: The poet (grandson) creates a bittersweet portrait of an old man in his last days in a nursing home. He characterizes the old man as someone who lived his married life according to his own rules, left all child-rearing responsibilities to his wife, drank too much, never saved his money, and never developed close relationships with his children. Despite these negative traits, the poet admires the old man, and to some extent even idealizes him, as someone who once lived a vital life and now has come to a pathetic end.

   In effect, his grandfather has been reduced to an *old* man— someone who is just another inmate in an institution. And now his wife dominates him in her nightly visits to the nursing home. She comes "hating the river" and "wearing the true faith / Like an iron nightgown." She stands over him with her children "ranged at her side, / Beating their little Bibles till he died."

Two other poems, "Grandmother Watching at Her Window" (1960) and "Grandmother's Dying" (1960), provide further insights into the character of the grandmother as depicted in "Grandfather in the Old Men's Home." In the first poem the old woman surveys her life and realizes that she was always saying goodbye to others. The image of her "watching at her window" becomes a metaphor for the losses she has experienced in her life. She turns to religion as a refuge from her pain, but the poet suggests that her faith has failed to resolve her loneliness. In the second poem her religious faith again is characterized as narrow and uncompromising. At the age of 93, she suffers a serious stroke and is cared for grudgingly by her family. She makes a pathetic picture, a tough old woman whose relationship with her family is superficial and even cold.

424　*Author:* O'Hehir, Diane
　　　Title: "Home Free." In **Home Free**. New York: Atheneum, 1988
　　　Genre: poem
　　　Commentary: An adult child realizes that she needs to find a meaningful way to say goodbye to her aged parent who is dying. The poet's father, 90, is confined to his bed in a nursing home. The old man appears to be comatose. His arms are "pulled up like bird's wings."

The poet finds an appropriate image that will justify the impending separation of father and daughter when she recalls the Buddhist tradition of releasing small birds at temples—as a means of symbolizing the soul's flight from one existence to another. She ends the poem with an image of that bird escaping from its cage—an appropriate image for the soul of her father that will be freed someday from its confinement in his broken-down body.

425　*Title:* "Shore"
　　　Commentary: This poem depicts a daughter's struggle to accept the gradual physical and mental decline of her father, 87. The poet compares the ups and downs of her father's bizarre behavior—the consequences of dementia—to the actions of a kite that soars, dips, and plunges as it is whipped by the wind. Although her father does not recognize her, she spends time with him and remains committed to their past relationship: "I love you / Because you're old, because you need me, because you look like / someone I am forgetting."

In "The Prayer Meeting at the Nursing Home" (1988), a daughter shares several bittersweet images from a visit to the nursing home where her father resides. The old man is weak, fearful, and disoriented. The prayer meeting is portrayed as a depressing and futile exercise for people who are lost in their private worlds.

426　*Author:* Pastan, Linda
　　　Title: "My Grandmother." In **The Five Stages of Grief: Poems by
　　　　　Linda Pastan**. New York: Norton, 1978
　　　Genre: poem
　　　Commentary: The poet recalls her Jewish grandmother, who married out of duty, not of love, and never resolved her feelings of anger

at having been forced to marry "the wrong man." She married "at her father's bidding" and tried to accept her fate. She expressed joy at the birth of her grandchildren, particularly her granddaughters. But when one of her granddaughters "married / a Gentile boy for love," the old woman covered her mirrors with black for seven days—as if to signify the death of someone in the family. The poet suggests that her bitter rejection of her granddaughter's marriage also reflects her own unresolved grief at having been compelled to marry someone she did not love. The poem ends with an ironic commentary: "she didn't see / her once beautiful face / wasted in the glass."

"Funerary Tower: Han Dynasty" portrays a mother and daughter's visit to the grave of the father. The mother appears to have resolved her feelings of grief for her husband, but the daughter, 40, is restless and impatient at the grave. She hurries her mother home. The speaker in "Old Woman" explains how she has learned to live with her griefs. In "The Five Stages of Grief," the longest poem in the book, the poet depicts grief as a circular process that does not promise easy resolution of one's loss. The poet relates her movement across the five stages: anger, denial, bargaining, depression, and acceptance. But at the end of the journey she concludes, "But something is wrong. / Grief is a circular staircase. / I have lost you."

427 *Author:* Ransom, John Crowe
   Title: "Old Man Playing with Children" (1923). In **Selected Poems**, 3rd ed. New York: Knopf, 1969
   Genre: poetry
   Commentary: In five short stanzas this poem dramatizes the point that the aging person should return to the child's naive openness to adventure and play.
   An old man is playing Indian with his grandsons. An adult onlooker, perhaps the parent of the boys, warns, "Watch grandfather, he'll set the house on fire." *House* and its attendant security is important to this speaker, who is appropriately identified not by relationship but only as "discreet householder."
   The poet, in the second stanza, undertakes to interpret the grandfather's thoughts. So, in the remaining three stanzas, the grandfather's real self speaks.
   What he says is that grandfather and grandson are "equally boy and boy." He rejects the "reclining-chair and slippers" of garrulous old age. He rejects those in middle age ("elder to these [boys] and

105

junior to me") whose energies are consumed by the material cares of
a safe life, who are so timid that even the noise of boys at play can
frighten them. The grandfather himself has lived through such an
unworthy adulthood, but now he resolves to be more "honorable" in
recognizing that "This life is not good but in danger and in joy."

This provocative theme leads naturally to discussion of what
kinds of "play" the aged person should seek beyond the children's
games that are the poem's symbol.

Another brief Ransom poem is "Piazza Piece" (1925), about a
lovesick old man who unhappily frightens a maiden, thus illustrat-
ing the conventional fear of sexuality in the old.

428 *Author:* Robinson, Edwin Arlington
   Title: "Isaac and Archibald" (1902). In **Selected Poems of Edwin
      Arlington Robinson.** Ed. by Morton Dauwen Zabel. New
      York: Macmillan, 1965
   Genre: poem
   Commentary: The serene awareness of oncoming decay and death
   is expressed in the friendship of two old men as witnessed by the
   speaker when a boy of twelve.
   This boy tags along with Isaac to visit Archibald, five miles out
   on a New England road on a hot summer day. Isaac tells him,

> A time will come to find out what it means
> To know that you are losing what was yours,
> To know that you are being left behind. . . .

The special pain of old age will be that of seeing "the best friend
of your life" go down in small collapses; this is what Isaac has seen
happening with his friend Archibald. Archibald, when they reach
his cottage, confides in the boy his similar fears for his friend Isaac.
Each old man shares with the boy his sober sadness at what is to
come; his faith that much good still remains in the last years; his be-
lief that if you "live to see clearly . . . the light will come to you, and
as you need it"; and his hope to be remembered as he is now. The
impressionable lad mingles their images with those legendary heroes he has read about. Later he still recalls them affectionately as
larger than life.
   A dozen pages long, this poem is deceptively prosy in its simple
language but eloquent in insights and suddenly luminous detail.

In "Mr. Flood's Party" (1921), a shorter poem from the same volume, a gentle old man holds a whimsical drinking party with himself on the way home at night.

429 *Author:* Roethke, Theodore
 Title: "Old Lady's Winter Words" (1953). In **The Collected Poems of Theodore Roethke**. Garden City, N.Y.: Doubleday, 1966
 Genre: poem
 Commentary: This two-page poem is an intense realization of the closing-down of old age in a woman who hungers for more life. She opens her soliloquy thus:

> To seize, to seize,—
> I know that dream.
> Now my ardors sleep in a sleeve.
> My eyes have forgotten.

The operative verb is "to seize," to make her own, to possess what is denied by her forgetful eyes and dimming ardors. She wants to hear a minstrel, perhaps a bird, sing of what's to come, to sing as "the marrow of God, talking." She would "hold high converse / Where the winds gather... / An old woman / Jumping in her shoes."

Her longing turns backward to the departed shine of her life, "When I went to sea in a sigh, / In a boat of beautiful things." These notes of ecstasy alternate with grief over all the sights and sounds that tell the passing of familiar things. She laments, "I have become a sentry of small seeds, / Poking alone in my garden." This alternation mounts until the arid grief of the closing lines, which open, "I fall, more and more, / Into my own silences."

Roethke's poetry is not easy. One sharp image, one sharp sensation, one sharp idea will give way abruptly to another, leaving the reader to intuit the hidden coherence. A longer poem (some 17 pages) is "Meditations of an Old Woman" (1958). Section 3 of the First Meditation treats vividly the clouded spiritual longings of old age. Section 4 expresses its marginal joys. A contrasting affirmation of joyous faith appears in the short late poem, "Once More, the Round" (1964).

430 *Author:* Sarton, May
     Title: "Gestalt at Sixty" (1972). In **Selected Poems of May Sarton.**
        Ed. by Serena Sue Hilsinger and Lois Byrnes. New York: Nor-
        ton, 1978
     Genre: poem
     Commentary: In this long poem Sarton charts the patterns of her
     existence that have contributed to the development of her self. The
     "gestalt" of her life includes the house she has lived in for ten years,
     her experience of the seasons, the garden that helped her survive her
     griefs, and the solitude that on the one hand "nourished" her and
     yet also "exposed" her to "moments of panic." She pauses at 60 to
     contemplate her aging. She concludes, "I am not ready to die, / But
     I am learning to trust death / As I have trusted life." She views her
     old age with optimism and embraces the change and suffering that
     is the basis of our existence.

431 *Title:* "On a Winter Night" (1953)
     Commentary: The poem is a meditation on the meaning of one's
     old age. Sarton begins with the perception of old age as a time of
     loss. She sits in front of the fire "in a cold room. . . feeling old." Ini-
     tially she mourns "the last fire of youth." Then she sees in the fire-
     light a sign of hope and regeneration. In the "first fire of age" she
     sees images of clarity, growth, seasoning, and rejuvenation.

     Sarton's poetry reflects her interest in the old person's develop-
     ment of self, the importance of "place" in the formation of identity,
     the role of solitude in one's experience, and the grieving process. In
     "Der Abschied [The Farewell]" (1961) the poet revisits a place that
     was important to her and to another person. Her memory of this re-
     lationship triggers a meditation on the temporary nature of all rela-
     tionships, the change that is a constant in our lives, and the
     recurring losses that we experience as we grow older.

     "Now I Become Myself" (1961) explores similar questions raised
     in "Gestalt at Sixty." In the former poem, Sarton suggests that the
     old person can experience a moment fusing all of the separate parts
     of her existence into an indivisible, organic whole. In "Of Grief"
     (1972), Sarton criticizes those who would neatly categorize grief re-
     sponses. She suggests that all responses to grief are unpredictable
     and idiosyncratic. Grief, like the substance of all human relation-
     ships, is more than the sum of its parts.

432 *Author:* Snyder, Gary
   Title: "Hay for the Horses." In **Riprap and Cold Mountain Poems**.
      San Francisco: Four Seasons Foundation, 1977
   Genre: poem
   Commentary: An old man of 68, in the midst of a still active life as
a laborer, takes the measure of his life in an unsentimental moment
of reflection. The lesson of the poem seems to be that people get
caught up in living their lives and don't realize—sometimes even until old age—that their lives have not turned out as they once had
thought.
   The old man had "driven half the night" to deliver a load of hay
to a California ranch. After hours of hard work helping to store the
hay in the barn, the old man joins the other laborers for lunch and
tells the men that he "first bucked hay" when he was 17. He recalls
thinking on that day 51 years earlier that he "sure would hate to do
this all my life." The poem ends with his chilling conclusion: "And
dammit, that's just what / I've gone and done." In other words, he
reveals with pained surprise that he has done little with his life.

433 *Author:* Tennyson, Alfred
   Title: "Ulysses" (1842). In **Alfred Tennyson: Poetical Works**. Lon-
      don: Oxford Univ. Pr., 1953
   Genre: poem
   Commentary: Rarely has such a thrilling call been voiced for old
age to keep on exploring life. The speaker is King Ulysses, a legendary hero of the Trojan War who spent nineteen years of epic adventure before reaching home in Ithaca. Now old, he is bored with the
routine duties of rulership. "I cannot rest from travel: I will drink /
Life to the lees." He speaks of himself as "this gray spirit yearning in
desire / To follow knowledge like a sinking star, / Beyond the ut-
most bound of human thought." So he will leave his throne for his
dutiful son Telemachus. He calls for his old sailors to make ready to
depart. They and he are still "One equal temper of heroic hearts, /
Made weak by time and fate, but strong in will / To strive, to seek,
to find, and not to yield." Tennyson's call can be heard by anyone
who might press forward into the late years—in science, art, learning, producing, travel, personal relationship.

   A contrasting poem, "Tithonus" (1860), dramatizes the vanity of
wanting to live forever. In Greek legend Tithonus was a handsome
youth loved by the goddess of the dawn. She granted him immortality but did not grant him perpetual youth as well; hence he aged and

aged until he begged for death. He is the speaker. The poem expresses his memories, his suffering, and his plea for release.

434   *Author:* Thomas, Dylan
       Title: "Do Not Go Gentle into That Good Night." In **Collected
            Poems, 1934–1952**. London: Dent, 1952
       Genre: poem
       Commentary: This well-known short poem, written as the poet's
       father was terminally ill, carries its theme in the title and opening
       line: Don't easily surrender to decline and death. "Old age should
       burn and rave at close of day."
          The next lines are intensely, elaborately constructed about four il-
       lustrations, all of persons who come to death knowing that they
       have missed full achievement in life. Wise men, knowing that their
       wisdom had failed to unleash "forked lightning," resist death. Good
       men, though their deeds never attained full brightness, resist death.
       "Wild men" (poets perhaps?), though their songs grieved that which
       they tried to celebrate, resist death. And so do "grave men," who
       learned too late that they might have witnessed the gaiety and blaze
       of life.
          So, in the final stanza, the speaker urges his father to resist "the
       dying of the light" and with the late wisdom of his "fierce tears" to
       bless and presumably inspire the poet.
          Literary readers will notice that this poem is a villanelle, a diffi-
       cult verse form using only two rhymes and only two stanza-closing
       lines, in alternation. The effect when it works is one of singing in-
       tensity.

435   *Author:* Tobias, John
       Title: "Reflections on a Gift of Watermelon Pickle Received from a
            Friend Called Felicity" (1961). In **Reflections on a Gift of Wa-
            termelon Pickle...and Other Modern Verse**. Comp. by
            Stephen Dunning and others. New York: Lothrop, 1967
       Genre: poem
       Commentary: The power of reminiscence to bring into the later
       years the delights of childhood is the theme of this clear and beauti-
       ful 45-line poem.
          The first three stanzas describe a magical summer long ago when
       "unicorns were still possible," when knees were skinned, chestnut
       pipes were smoked, and, above all, when "watermelons ruled" with
       their endless bites of cold sweetness.
          A short transitional stanza states that "the bites are fewer now," to
       be enjoyed only as rare and transient. But, as the final stanza states,

a jar of watermelon pickles has been preserved by "Felicity." When tasted, "unicorns become possible again." Even though that ancient summer "maybe never was" as wonderful as remembered, its restorative grace makes it more real than any actual summer.

The "Felicity" who gave the jar of pickles may be taken as an actual friend or perhaps, as the name implies, Happiness itself—the felicity of a good young life that lays aside its memories to be tasted later.

436 *Author:* Van Doren, Mark
   Title: "The First Snow of the Year" (1963). In **Collected and New Poems: 1924–1963**. New York: Hill & Wang, 1963
   Commentary: This ten-stanza narrative poem depicts a brief interchange between an old couple in their house while outside "the first snow of the year danced on the lawn." The poem begins with the old man, possibly bedridden, listening to his wife bringing him a tray with some warm milk. He hears her steps on the stairs, and when he hears the snow "peppering the panes," he is stirred by a memory of their courting. Both are united in this important memory. As the season turns (the first snow), so does the old man's life decline. The metaphor of the first snow of the season suggests their inevitable separation. Yet the poem affirms the power of love that endures through a long relationship. The old couple are soothed by the sweetness of this memory.

437 *Title:* "We Were Not Old" (1937)
   Genre: poem
   Commentary: The fate of an old man who lives alone is considered by a group of young people while a blizzard rages outside their house. What do the young think about this old man? They pity him, feel that he shouldn't have to survive such an onslaught, and conclude, "He should have died . . . some pretty summer."

The poet corrects these conclusions by stating, "Each of us here could think this, and be wrong." Why? The simple answer is, "We were not old. We had not loved the winter . . . ." This old man has valued the "meanness" of the natural elements; love and anger have helped him to adapt to harsh circumstances; he has "learned to measure life by blows." This old man has been most alive when he has had something to bear up against.

Other poems reprinted in *Collected and New Poems* worth noting: "Spirit" (1924) celebrates an old woman who maintains her mental and physical well-being through the routine of preparing tea.

"His Trees" (1937) likens an old man to the old trees in a grove he has nurtured all of his life. "Death of Old Men" (1928) is a eulogy of sorts, intended to illustrate how much is lost from the world when old men die. A similar tone is evoked in "Envy the Old" (1953) when the old, who have stepped aside from active involvement from life and become "those sitters by the wall," are praised for their "stillness" and "silence." In "Age Is Age" (1944) the perfect image of old age—"mythical old man"—is shown to be an unrealizable image. The best that one can hope for is to make peace with one's old age and death.

438 *Author:* Wagoner, David
      Title: "Part Song" (1976). In **In Broken Country: Poems** by David
            Wagoner. Boston: Little, 1979
      Commentary: Old age has come to this: residents of a nursing home
      and their families gathered for a pathetic Thanksgiving party. The
      poet sets the scene to convey some sense of how the old are patron-
      ized. Accompanied by "tea and cookies and clumsy conversation,"
      the janitor sings the sentimental favorite "Trees" (based on the Joyce
      Kilmer poem) in "a heart-failed baritone." Wagoner puts readers in
      touch with their own darkest fears about old age, particularly with
      the deadening experience of life in a nursing home. The old people
      in his poem are immobile, detached, waiting for death. The family
      members at the Thanksgiving party are caught up in their private
      memories of personal losses. Nobody connects. Readers will be able
      to identify with the somber, even despairing tone of resignation in
      the poem.

439 *Title:* "Into the Nameless Places" (1978).
      Genre: poem
      Commentary: Wagoner takes us into the mind of an old woman in a
      nursing home who suffers from a dementia. The poem is structured
      around six questions that are meant to orient her to reality—e.g.,
      "The date is?" "The weather is?" As each question is posed, the old
      woman responds primarily through an interior monologue that re-
      veals her confusion and desperation.
          The poem's images speak of decline, loss, and fearfulness. For
      this old person, reality is a state of existence that is "slipping away,"
      "out of reach, beyond me, without me." Although her behavior sug-
      gests that she is suffering from serious mental confusion, her inte-
      rior monologue demonstrates that she is in contact with a strange
      inner landscape peopled with fragments of memories. She can find
      no way to communicate that personal reality to the questioner. She

fails the reality orientation test. The ending lines of the poem illustrate her despair: "and no one / Asks out of politeness why I stare at nothing / As if it were really there."

440 *Author:* Warren, Robert Penn

Title: "Ballad of Your Puzzlement." In **Being Here: Poetry 1977–1980**. New York: Random, 1980

Genre: poem

Commentary: In an afterword to this book of poems, Warren refers to this poem as a means of introducing the concluding section, which is "concerned with the reviewing of life from the standpoint of age." He concludes with this statement: "Indeed, it may be said that our lives are our own supreme fiction."

This idea is at the core of the poem. Warren suggests that as we grow older we know ourselves less and less. We play back our lives like movies, but the main character of the movie is "a hero strange to you / And a plot you can't understand." In the poem he plays back several plots, each with a different hero. Finally, he asks, "Yes, how many names has Truth? / Yes, how many lives have you lived?" The poet acknowledges the multiplicity of truths and lies that each of us live. He does not reproach us for our faults; he invites us to welcome, accept, and celebrate the complexity, and even perhaps the incomprehensibility of our identities. After the title of the poem he adds a parenthetical statement that may be taken as an admonition for what follows: "(How not to recognize yourself as what you think you are, when old and reviewing your life before death comes)."

In "Safe in Shade" the poet recalls his childhood. He loved to listen to an old man who "sat in his big chair propped / Against reddish tatter of / Bole-bark of the great cedar." Then he was "Safe in the bourne of distance and shade," safe from the complications and burdens associated with growing up. Now in old age the poet wonders where he can find a similar respite from the pressures of daily life. In part of a longer poem, "Synonyms," Warren depicts "a grubby old dame" who overcomes her physical limitations and rescues a kitten from its tormenter.

441 *Author:* Wheelock, John Hall

Title: "Song on Reaching Seventy" (1956). In **The Gardener and Other Poems**. New York: Scribner, 1961

Genre: poem

Commentary: The preciousness of life as it can appear to an older person is celebrated in this poem, spoken in solitude. Just as a thrush may lift up its heart against the night, so the speaker may sing as he looks into the greater night of death. Every detail of nature is now seen in piercing beauty and longing. So is every tender memory, until the speaker feels "joy that is almost pain, pain that is joy, / Unimaginable to younger man or boy." The poem ends with a prayer for just a little more of this joy before waking "out of the dream of self into the truth of all, / The price for which is death."

Wheelock, who wrote much of his poetry in old age, is a graceful and cultured poet who in several other poems on aging expresses a sensitive and loving attitude toward nature and the people around him. "Night Thoughts in Age" (*Poems Old and New*; Scribner, 1956) shows the speaker, lying awake in the seaside home he has lived in from childhood, as he listens to the "music" of his life—the memories, the terrors, the blessings. In doing so he finds reconcilement with his mortality. "Sentimental Monologue at Seventy" from the same volume is a wry quatrain in which the wise old speaker wishes he could console himself as he did when a sorrowing young man.

In "The Gardener" (1957; *The Gardener and Other Poems*), the aged speaker stands in the park-like estate left by his father. He appreciates that gift as well as the parent's love of woodland beauty, his care in bringing this love to visible form in the surrounding trees, gardens, and lawns. The speaker of "Return in Age" from the same volume stands by the sea. He poignantly remembers his "first love, young love, wild love," and wishes she might return.

442   *Author:* Whitman, Walt
       Title: "Song at Sunset" (1860). In **Leaves of Grass**, comprehensive
          edition. Ed. by Harold W. Blodgett and Sculley Bradley. New
          York: New York Univ. Pr., 1965
       Genre: poem
       Commentary: Whitman's poetry, collected under the title *Leaves of Grass*, is one great celebration of America and American life in all its variety, including old age. It is also a celebration of Whitman himself, not as a private person but as the voice and embodiment of America. "I sing myself," as he said in many ways.
          "Song of Sunset" speaks of the beauty of day's end and implicitly of life's end. Stanza after stanza utters a great joy at everything life brings, at the

Good in all,
In the satisfaction and aplomb of animals,
In the annual return of the seasons,
In the hilarity of youth,
In the strength and flush of manhood,
In the grandeur and exquisiteness of old age,
In the superb vistas of death.

This abundant praise ends:

O setting sun! though the time has come,
I still warble under you, if none else does, unmitigated adoration.

Whitman did find old age difficult at times, as in "Queries to My Seventieth Year" (1888), in which he asks whether the coming year will "leave me as now, / Dull, parrot-like and old, with crack'd voice harping, screeching?" But his essential confidence runs through several brief poems as they address old age. "Youth, Day, Old Age and Night" (1858) puts the question to youth in all its powers: "Do you know that Old Age may come after you with equal grace, force, fascination?" "Now Finale to the Shore" (1871) cheerfully commands the old person (the speaker himself) to bid farewell to "land and life" and "obey thy cherish'd secret wish" and "depart upon thy endless cruise Old Sailor." "Old Age's Lambent Peaks" (1888) likens the splendor of high peaks catching the last sunlight to the final glory and wisdom of old age. "Old Age's Ship and Crafty Death's" (1890) expresses the determination to outspeed those two pursuers and "take to the deepest, freest waters." Whitman published this poem when he was 70 and in poor health.

443 *Author:* Williams, William Carlos
    Title: "Asphodel, That Greeny Flower" (1955). In **The Collected Poems of William Carlos Williams,** vols. 1 and 2. Ed. by Christopher MacGowan. New York: New Directions, 1988
    Genre: poem
    Commentary: Williams wrote this poem in old age, addressing his wife of forty years and celebrating their long love. The poem itself is long (27 pages); it is a major work by a major American poet of much complexity. It can most readily show its rich splendor to readers with some experience in modern verse.

    The poem consists of three "books" and a coda. The central image is the asphodel, a fragile flower, which comes early to announce spring (it was also said to bloom in hell), that the poet collected as a boy, and that comes through a series of expansions to symbolize the universal redeeming and immortal power of love and imagination. Secondary images that blend into the poem: the sea, primal source of life and beauty; blind Homer, singer of the sea and father of poetry; the nuclear bomb, flower and symbol of death and suppression; and light, which comes before the thunderclap and represents all love in the shadow of death.

The aged speaker above all tells his wife of the forgiveness he has needed. This forgiveness is the very nature of love and is now strengthening that love. After reflecting over their long marriage and many intense events in his own life, he ends with the wedding by which they had begun. Here the asphodel is climactically compared to "an odor from our wedding / [which] has revived for me / and begun again to penetrate / into all crevices / of my world."

Williams wrote many shorter, more accessible poems on themes of aging. "To Waken an Old Lady" (1921) likens old age to a flight of small birds that find contentment in midwinter in a field of broken seedhusks. "The Widow's Lament in Springtime" (1921) voices the piercing sorrow of losing a long-time spouse at a time when the world is bursting into flower. In "To a Poor Old Woman" (1935) is seen the consuming and comforting joy of small pleasures in an old woman munching plums. "The Centenarian" (1933) celebrates the pleasure of an extremely old lady in receiving a whiskey toast from her friends. In "The Last Words of My English Grandmother" (1938), a feisty old woman is moved noisily from her untidy lodgings to an ambulance, where she utters her final words of tired wisdom.

444 *Author:* Yeats, William Butler
   Title: "The Wild Swans at Coole" (1919). In **W. B. Yeats: The**
      Poems. Ed. by Richard J. Finneran. New York: Collier, 1989
   Genre: poem
   Commentary: In a haunting vision of the streaming away of youth into old age, Yeats explores one way that timeless beauty compensates for the changes effected by time and circumstance. Standing by the water at Coole on a still October day, the narrator looks out upon 59 swans. He recalls that 19 years have passed since he first saw these swans appear. At first, he responds with sadness at the thought of how much has changed in his life in those 19 years. But he realizes that the swans represent something eternal and mysterious: "Their hearts have not grown old." He acknowledges that even

when the swans depart from Coole, they will offer their grace and beauty to others.

445 *Title:* "Sailing to Byzantium" (1928)
Commentary: This well-known poem contains one of the most eloquent expressions of Yeats' often-felt dismay and rage at aging: "An aged man is but a paltry thing, / A tattered coat upon a stick." Turning away from the sensual world of the young, the aged speaker declares, "That is no country for old men. The young / In one another's arms, birds in the trees / . . . Fish, flesh, or fowl, commend all summer long / Whatever is begotten, born and dies." He turns instead to "the holy city of Byzantium," by which is meant the ancient city of everlasting works of art. There he will devote himself to art that is timeless and be gathered "Into the artifice of eternity."

446 *Title:* "The Wild Old Wicked Man" (1938)
Commentary: Here is an exuberant celebration of sexuality in aging. Two voices are heard in this dialogue, which has the flavor and cryptic refrain of an old ballad. The wild old man begs a pious woman to give him love, because he is still "mad about women" and can pierce their hearts with the words and wit denied to younger men. The woman replies that all her love has been given to God, "the old man in the skies."

The personas in Yeats' poems often reflect bitterly on the changes that are wrought by the effects of time. "The Lamentation of the Old Pensioner" (1893) shows a lonely old man recalling the women and political excitement of former days; he ends with the defiant curse: "I spit in the face of Time / That has transfigured me." The character Aengus in "The Song of Wandering Aengus" (1899) tries to recapture the perfect love he experienced in the past. In "An Acre of Grass" (1938), Yeats rages at old age in an attempt to recover his imagination and vitality. "Grant me an old man's frenzy, / Myself must I remake / Till I am Timon and Lear." In these lines Yeats refers to characters who learned to understand themselves by raging at their folly and ill fortune. Yeats portrays his long-standing desire to recover the powers of imagination and creativity against the onslaught of time and age in "A Prayer for Old Age" (1935). He ends the poem with a fervent cry for a response to life that will redeem his soul: "I pray. . . / That I may seem, though I die old, / A foolish, passionate man."

Nonfiction

501 *Author:* Beauvoir, Simone de
Title: **The Coming of Age** (1970). Trans. by Patrick O'Brian. New York: Putnam, 1978
Genre: nonfiction
Commentary: Few books can offer such an education in aging as this masterwork by a prominent French intellectual. Declaring her intention "to break the conspiracy of silence" about the aged, Beauvoir more than puts silence to flight. She draws upon almost every major field of inquiry to explore aging in its fullest dimensions.

Part I, Old Age as Seen from Without, traces the history of Western gerontological thought from Egyptian to present times. Then ethnology and anthropology are brought in to show the place of old age in different cultures past and recent, from nonliterate peoples to literate, from Eastern to Western. Old Age in Present-Day Society closes Part I.

An important generalization on this point is that old age enjoys most importance in societies that are strongly organized and repetitive, thus stabilizing the role of the aged, at the same time valuing their experience in tasks that are ongoing. Old age enjoys least importance in societies that are troubled or revolutionary, when traditional rank and experience lose their value—this being the case in our own times of rapid technological and cultural change.

Part II, The Being-in-the-World, looks at old age as subjective experience, beginning with what variously happens to body and mind in the aging process. How do people understand their own aging and oncoming death? What functions are performed by memory? What careers and other pursuits are successfully followed in old age? (Beauvoir's analysis of aging in different occupations is especially fascinating.) How do old people relate to current trends and events? In the last major chapter, Old Age and Everyday Life, Beauvoir considers the special emotional attitudes among older people, the many depressive aspects of the late years as well as such advantages as freedom from responsibility and hypocrisy, as well as the more promising lines of continued vitality.

Beauvoir's Conclusion drives home the indictment that she evidently felt at the outset, that Westerners live in a society that "cares about the individual only in so far as he is profitable." Although old age may be pleasant enough for the affluent who have health, leisure, and developed tastes to enjoy it, it imposes a grinding misery upon the subjugated worker "whose meaning of his existence has been stolen from him from the very beginning." Only a radical reconstruction of society can remove the lifelong exploitation of people that renders their old age so crushing. Then, says Beauvoir, we may "go on pursuing ends that give our lives a meaning."

This summary hardly does justice to the breadth and vividness of Beauvoir's illustration throughout. She draws from literature, art, politics, biography, history, from her personal life. One cannot easily skip through her ample discussions of old age in such giants as Victor Hugo, Michelangelo, Verdi, Freud, Churchill, and Chateaubriand. Beauvoir's style is only occasionally abstruse. For the most part it is clear, serious, informed throughout by a vast mastery of subject and a thoroughly humane spirit. Anyone intending to explore gerontology could hardly do better than to start with this work as a splendid overture to the subject.

502 *Author:* Beauvoir, Simone de
Title: **A Very Easy Death** (1964). Trans. by Patrick O'Brian. New York: Putnam, 1965
Genre: nonfiction
Commentary: Beauvoir's memoir is a graphic depiction of her mother's prolonged suffering and eventual death from cancer over a six-week period. Beauvoir captures the full range of her mother's response to her illness: fear, anger, denial, uncertainty, defiance, courage, loneliness, and acceptance. Beauvoir also analyzes the contradictions that were the essence of her mother's character, and she reflects upon the ambivalence of their mother-daughter relationship.

In an early chapter Beauvoir provides some perspective on her mother's unhappy childhood, her unfulfilled marriage, and her devotion to her daughters, Simone and Poupette. Maman, as they affectionately called her, often felt both "guilty and misunderstood." Beauvoir documents the long-standing antagonisms between her mother and herself. Her mother never accepted Beauvoir's lack of religious faith, her controversial social and political views, or her long-term relationship with Jean Paul Sartre, whom she never married. Beauvoir concludes, "So we each paralyzed the other."

More contradictions appear in Beauvoir's and her sister's responses to their mother's struggle. Beauvoir writes, "What tried us more than anything were Maman's death-agonies, her resurrections, and our own inconsistency." The daughters were appalled at the magnitude of their mother's suffering. They even considered euthanasia as an alternative to a series of operations. Yet they were impressed by their mother's unyielding courage in the face of unbearable pain and were heartened each time she survived a crisis.

One of the nurses characterizes Maman's death as "a very easy death." The irony of this phrase is self-evident; Beauvoir's mother experienced repeated moments of intense pain and agony. But her death was eased, to some extent, because she received excellent nursing care, was treated in a fine hospital, was visited daily by one of her daughters, and did not die alone.

503   *Author:* Blythe, Ronald
      Title: **The View in Winter: Reflections on Old Age.** New York: HBJ, 1979
      Genre: nonfiction
      Commentary: Some forty voices of older English people are recorded in this masterpiece of oral history done in the 1970s. If their times are long gone, their experience and wisdom remain—wide-ranging and immediate in effect. Their present and former vocations span the population: mining, soldiering, farming, homekeeping, medicine, teaching, ministry, and gentry. Ronald Blythe, who must have combined a tape recorder with a sensitive ear, lets us hear them in their own dialects, idioms, slang, and humor.

The rural village and its aged fill the first of eight sections. Here Blythe finds not only the elderly who have retired to the countryside but also those ancient villagers who recall an older culture of aged neglect. A second section brings out relationships between old and young. A heartening conversation among older schoolchildren is included, full of good humor and honest observation of the older people they know. In the section The Old People's Home, we hear the very old as they cope with the closing-in world of the county institution.

How old people take their lifelong stamp from great motions of history is illustrated by two sections, one on the First World War and one on the early struggle of Welsh miners against the coal masters. Such stimuli magnetize the whole lifetimes of the survivors but also isolate them from later generations. In the same way, the old feel lost as their "references" vanish—the fashions, manners, ideologies, social positions, and people who gave orientation to their formative years. The needs to talk and to "get about" fill two other sections. The volume closes with the moving testimonies of religious people of their faith in the last years.

Blythe's own commentary enlightens the reader fully as much as do his interviews. He writes lucidly, he is well read in the literature of aging, he is compassionate without sentimentality. His own language and that of his people resonate with insights: "Perhaps, with full-span lives the norm, people may need to learn how to be aged as they once had to learn to be adult." "The aged and the young. . . wail because they are dead serious in a world which finds them either too young or too old to take seriously." "I wish I had this much brains when I was younger." "Old men like to eavesdrop on the work they have left."

504 *Author:* Butler, Robert N.

Title: **Why Survive? Being Old in America**. New York: Harper, 1975

Genre: nonfiction

Commentary: This landmark resource treats almost every problem and potential of the aging process. Its statistics, though outdated, retain general force; the discussion remains wholly current.

Dr. Butler, a psychiatrist and gerontologist, opens by saying, "Aging is the neglected stepchild of the human life cycle." (In 1968 he himself had coined the term "ageism" for the widespread prejudice against the elderly.) After reviewing the myths and stereotypes by which old age is misunderstood and mistreated, he takes up, chapter by chapter, the real needs of the aging as to income, employment, living arrangements, medical and psychiatric care, terminal arrangements.

Such a huge new constituency as America's aged imposes both needs and conflicts upon the electorate. In this book direction is given through Butler's outlines of goals for private activism and public policy. The national goal should be "not simply the extension of life but the creation of a healthy, vigorous, self-productive old age."

America has so rigidly compartmentalized the life cycle—into education for the young, work for the middle years, and retirement for the old—that many people reach old age unprepared. A broader education continued throughout life will encourage the interests and capacities by which the late years can be rich and active. This is the message of the final chapters. The book ends by calling for "a new sensibility" about aging, to be instilled through literature and the arts. (AGING IN LITERATURE is one response to that call.)

505 *Author:* Comfort, Alex
     Title: **A Good Age**. Illustrated by Michael Leonard. New York:
        Crown, 1976
     Genre: nonfiction
     Commentary: This text is a compendium of about 75 terms divided
     evenly between two categories: biological aging and social gerontol-
     ogy. (Comfort uses the term "sociogenic" aging, which he defines as
     the "role which society imposes on people as they reach a certain
     chronologic age.") Comfort is an advocate for the rights of the el-
     derly; he abhors the ageist stereotypes that render the old useless,
     worn-out, expendable "unpeople."
          He wants older people to take control of their aging process and
     change what they can about the negative stereotypes associated
     with aging. He wants the old to fight ageism just as other minorities
     have struggled against racism. He concludes, "So long as society is
     what it is, self-defense is the main skill people need as they get
     older." He charts numerous examples of the obstacles that the old
     must overcome to maintain their dignity, self-respect, health, and
     social standing.
          Comfort's writing style is straightforward and intimate. He ad-
     dresses the reader as "you" and avoids highly technical explanations
     of complicated topics. He is adept at turning a phrase. Some exam-
     ples: On "senility": "Old people go crazy for three reasons—
     because of illness, because they were always crazy, or because we
     drive them crazy." On "euthanasia": "As a rule euthanasia is what
     the relatives clamor for." On hobbies: "We haven't gone deeply into
     hobbies here. We prefer occupation." On retirement: "Two weeks is
     about the ideal length of time to retire."
          The text is complemented by more than 50 illustrations of older
     people and brief paragraphs highlighting their achievements. Most
     of these people are entertainers, artists, writers, and politicians—
     George Burns, Michelangelo, Tolstoy, De Gaulle. A few are repre-
     sentative older people who excelled in old age.

506 *Author:* Cowley, Malcolm
     Title: **The View from 80**. New York: Viking, 1980
     Genre: nonfiction
     Commentary: Cowley, a literary scholar, wrote this 75-page essay
     when he turned 80. His essay addresses the following questions:
     How does the coming of age affect the individual? What can one ex-
     pect from life after reaching 80? Who has written about the experi-
     ence of old age from the perspective of the old person? Cowley
     offers a personal account of his aging, and he provides some histori-

cal perspectives, gerontological data, and case studies of individual responses to old age. He also summarizes the contributions of Florida Scott-Maxwell, Cicero, Alex Comfort, and Simone de Beauvoir, all of whom wrote extensively on the experience of old age.

Cowley writes, "To enter the country of age is a new experience, different from what you supposed it to be. Nobody, man or woman, knows the country until he has lived in it and taken out his citizenship papers." The aging person learns to recognize physical symptoms and societal messages that communicate the message "You are old." Still, the person who is 80 feels that "the true, essential self is ageless."

Cowley notes some of the more unfortunate responses to aging: avarice, untidiness, and vanity. But he insists that the old can find pleasure in solitude and stillness, simple satisfactions, and reminiscences. He concludes, "The people I envy are those who accept old age as a series of challenges." His advice to those who are aging is consistent with this conclusion: he suggests that the best antidote to the negative consequences of old age is to maintain a level of activity that will keep one interested in and involved in the opportunities of old age.

507 *Author:* Fischer, David H.
 Title: **Growing Old in America**. New York: Oxford Univ. Pr., 1977
 Genre: nonfiction
 Commentary: As Professor Fischer points out, "The experience of aging itself has changed faster than our understanding of it. [It] is an experience profoundly different today from what it was two or three centuries ago." In this brief history, he makes a lucid and well-illustrated effort to trace its history in America.

Chapter I, The Exaltation of Age in Early America: 1607–1820, explains how older citizens (men especially) were revered, given precedence, and listened to. Chapter II, The Revolution in Age Relations: 1770–1820, shows a deep shift whereby the aged were displaced in influence. Wealth carried more weight as its extremes widened. New concepts of liberty and equality reduced the deference given to the old.

The numerous forces that led to a radical demotion of age are outlined in Chapter III, The Cult of Youth in Modern America: 1780–1970. Examples: "young" movements in politics, the rapid outdating of knowledge, the dispersion of the extended family, mandatory retirement, the ascendance of youth culture. One bright note has been the increased affection between the generations in place of the authority of parents and grandparents. Reducing the importance of age has been accompanied by large increases in the numbers of aged as well as in their life spans. America's response to the resulting tensions is addressed by Chapter IV, Old Age Becomes a Social Problem: 1909–1970. It explains the rise of government concern for the aged, the pension movement including Social Security, geriatric medicine, and gerontology.

A final chapter, A Thought for the Future, proposes that Americans should reject both the worship of age (*gerontophilia*) and the fear of age (*gerontophobia*). Instead, they should move toward *gerontophratria*: "a fraternity of age and youth, a brotherhood of generations." This accord will not come, however, as long as either generation must depend on the other—an unhappy feature of present Social Security financing. As one solution, the author puts forward a national fiscal plan of his own. He ends by arguing that the work ethic that has motivated so much of American life be joined by other ethics of "being" that can dignify and enrich the more inactive phases of life.

What makes Professor Fischer's book more than merely clear and informative is his ingenuity with evidence. How do we really *know* how old age was regarded in other times? To find out, he and his colleagues have examined old census reports; records of precedence in church seating; rosters of public leadership; treatments of old age in portraiture, costume, language, inheritance customs, and so on. Instances are liberally, even entertainingly, cited.

508 *Author:* Honel, Rosalie Walsh
Title: **Journey with Grandpa: Our Family's Struggle with Alzheimer's Disease.** Baltimore: Johns Hopkins Univ. Pr., 1988
Genre: nonfiction
Commentary: When Frank Honel, 80, began to exhibit the signs of Alzheimer's disease, his son Milt and daughter-in-law Rosalie began to care for him in their home. That decision led to a seven-year commitment on their part as Frank's condition declined. The effects of Alzheimer's disease are recreated honestly and sometimes graphically in this book. The family was faced with Frank's repetitive meaningless dialogue, his incessant wandering, his angry outbursts, and his incontinence. These bizarre behaviors became part of the family's daily routine.

This book chronicles the emotional and psychological toll exacted by their commitment. Rosalie was the primary caregiver, but all members of the family experienced frustration, resentment, guilt feelings, jealousies, grief, and despair. At the same time, they discovered wellsprings of creativity by adapting to Frank's needs, learned the limits of their family's endurance, and accepted—to the best of their ability—the responsibilities of treating Frank as a whole person.

Why didn't the Honels put Frank in a nursing home as the disease progressed? Throughout this ordeal they tried to strike a balance between the rigors of caring for the old man and the sense that they were accepting responsibility, making a contribution, and finding a measure of understanding and resolution through their efforts. Both Rosalie and Milt conclude that their care resolved personal and family relationships and gave them a new appreciation of their family, their mutual love, and their personal faith.

509 *Author:* Jury, Mark, and Dan Jury
Title: **Gramp: A Man Ages and Dies.** New York: Viking, 1976
Genre: nonfiction
Commentary: In this photographic essay, Mark and Dan Jury portray the gradual mental and physical decline and eventual death of their grandfather, Frank Tugend, known affectionately as "Gramp." On the one hand, Frank Tugend is a statistic—one of several million people each year who suffer from a disease that affects their mental functioning. But in the text, Gramp is not a statistic. He is shown in an early section, Family Album, as a child, young married man, father, and grandfather. He is vital, engaged, happy-go-lucky. He is in robust health. These photographs provide an important counterpoint to the confused, fearful old man shown in later images. Throughout the text, readers are given insights into one family's attempts to respect Gramp's dignity and character despite the problems associated with his mental and physical decline.

At first the family is shocked when Gramp begins to suffer lapses of memory and periods of confusion, which are diagnosed by the family physician as evidence of organic brain syndrome. When his condition worsens, the family decides to take care of him at home rather than place him in an institution. More than 100 photographs graphically depict the old man's progressive decline and document the family's trials as round-the-clock caregivers.

One day Gramp pulls out his false teeth, hands them to Dan, and tells him that he won't need them anymore. Soon he slips into a coma. The photographs of the death watch are expressive of the family's love for Gramp. Three generations of family members interact with Gramp during the final days of his life.

510 *Author:* Koch, Kenneth
   Title: **I Never Told Anybody: Teaching Poetry Writing in a Nursing Home.** New York: Vintage, 1978
   Genre: nonfiction
   Commentary: Koch, an accomplished poet and teacher, recounts his experience in teaching poetry to 25 residents in the American Nursing Home in New York City in 1976. Working with poet Kate Farrell, Koch discovered that writing poetry increased the older people's self-confidence and stimulated their latent creativity. At first, some of the students had to overcome negative attitudes about poetry writing. But after they discovered that they *could* write poetry, they learned to love it and began to respond to and even analyze their own and other's work. Koch learned that some of his stereotypes about old people were inappropriate. His students were not preoccupied with nostalgia, and they had not lost touch with the intensity of their emotional lives. They were willing to confront ambivalent feelings and speak directly and openly about significant personal experiences through their poetry.

   Koch's approach succeeded because he taught poetry as an art form, rather than using it as a means of therapy. He organized classes around topics, such as colors, music, touch, seasons, and comparisons. Some of his more creative ideas: quiet (remember the quietest time in your life), talking to the moon and stars (the poet addresses the natural world), lies (everything the poet writes is a lie), and "I never told anybody" (personal self-disclosures). Koch taught the students a poetry that emphasizes concreteness, specificity, and control of the poetic line. Rhyming was discouraged.

   The book is divided into two parts: Koch's overview of the experience, and a summary of 18 lesson plans. The latter section includes representative student poems written during the class. The creativity, imagination, humor, and insight of the old is amply documented. Readers get to know some of the poets who found their voices through the medium of poetry. The text will likely stimulate readers to discover the possibilities of writing their own poetry.

511 *Author:* Lax, Eric
   Title: "The Death of My Father." In **The Atlantic Monthly**, 242:75–78 (July 1978)
   Genre: nonfiction
   Commentary: In this reminiscence, Eric Lax reviews the last months of his father's life and reveals the strong intergenerational bond that existed between them. Jack Lax, an Episcopal minister, is characterized as a humorous, loving man who integrated the values of toler-

ance, compassion, and faith into the fabric of his life and passed those values on to his son. Eric explains the basis of their relationship simply: "I liked my father a lot. He was funny and warm and does not seem to have burdened me with much of the excess baggage parents sometimes heap on their children."

Eric Lax provides insights into his father's past: he recalls his father's love of practical jokes, his dedication to the ministry, and his harsh experiences in the Depression. When Eric learned that his father had cancer, Eric began to spend more time with him, a response he characterizes as "an unsurprising decision." Lax writes descriptively about the interactions between father and son: Eric telling his father the news that the cancer is inoperable, Jack giving his son a few words of advice when he realizes he is dying, Eric rushing to the hospital and arriving just in time to hold his father in his arms as the old man dies.

These interactions allow the two to speak honestly about their feelings for each other without becoming sentimental. Even Lax's description of the funeral reflects the sense of completeness and resolution that is the hallmark of his father's life.

512 *Author:* Olmstead, Alan H.
    Title: **Threshold: The First Days of Retirement**. New York: Harper, 1975
    Genre: nonfiction
    Commentary: Threshold is an excellent document for understanding the first shocks and some of the opportunities of retirement. It is the journal of the first six months of retirement, kept by a New England editor who retired at 65 rather than work under new management.

Olmstead's first entry, September 4, 1972, opens: "I have no job to go to tomorrow morning, and I am frightened." His final entry, March 14, 1973, closes: "The most frequent thought I have had in this first half year is that I should have begun doing this a long time ago." In between, he is concerned with the nature of retirement. He works his way through the anxiety of not being vocationally needed and not feeling financially secure to the satisfactions of watching nature, of reminiscing, of enjoying friends, and of acquiring a new independence.

He learns "the great retirement sin"—"of filling the day more and more easily with less and less." He joins his wife in housework. He takes satisfaction in the handyman jobs that pit this former editor against the brute antagonism of refractory plumbing and unpruned

trees. He takes a new look at the career in which he felt so important, a new look at patriotism, a new look at war and peace.

His entries are short, seldom more than one page. In effect, they
resemble the newspaper columns that Olmstead wrote as a second
vocation, and they can be enjoyed wherever the reader opens the
book. The writing is clear, sensitive, candid. This book is not a profound analysis of aging but a personal account by a decent and ob-
servant person who finds retirement a new country to explore.

513   *Author:* Painter, Charlotte
      Title: **Gifts of Age: Portraits and Essays of 32 Remarkable Women**.
         Photography by Pamela Valois. San Francisco: Chronicle Bks.,
         1985
      Genre: nonfiction
      Commentary: Thirty-two women of different cultures, faiths, and
      ethnic backgrounds are celebrated in this coffee-table–sized book.
      The "gifts of age" of the title refers to the contributions that these
      older women have made to society through new careers, volunteer
      activities, and intergenerational relationships. Their stories illus-
      trate how one's creativity can blossom in old age.

      The subjects in the text possess a variety of talents; some of the
      women featured include a bellringer, a French chef, a potter, a
      speech therapist, a senior activist, a bookbinder, and a dancer.
      Most of the women are between 75 and 90 years old. Each of the
      women is introduced by a few paragraphs of text and a glossy black-
      and-white photograph on a separate page. These images of old age
      reflect the wisdom, beauty, and self-confidence of the subjects.
      Each is shown in a context that reveals individuating characteristics.
      The essays that follow, about 2,000 words each, usually tell stories
      about how the women's values were formed, how they practiced
      coping skills, what interpersonal relationships mattered most to
      them, and what they have learned in their lives.

      A few quotes may suggest the richness of some of their collective
      wisdom: One woman says, "I don't feel any difference in ages unless
      people just seem awfully old and creaky or awfully young and im-
      mature." Another woman refers to her grandmother's habit of plant-
      ing two rows of everything in her garden—"one for the family and
      one for anybody." One woman's secret is to maintain a perspective
      on one's activities: "If you can go out without being noticed and still
      do something worthwhile, that is happiness."

      Some of the women featured in the text are well known: author
      M. F. K. Fisher, television personality Julia Child, and Tish Som-
      mers, founder of the Older Woman's League.

514 *Author:* Sarton, May
Title: **At Seventy: A Journal**. New York: Norton, 1984
Genre: nonfiction
Commentary: This journal spans Sarton's seventieth year, beginning with an entry on the anniversary of her birth, May 3, 1982. The main theme in the journal is her desire to strike a balance between her need for solitude and the stimulus of social contacts. To Sarton, solitude is respite from the demands of her social calendar; it provides renewal of her personal energies, and the context in which she completes her writing projects. At one point she characterizes solitude as a means of "resuming her self." But social contacts contribute to her sense of self, too. In one entry she names the priorities in her life: "first friends, then work, then the garden."

The utility of Sarton's journal is not limited because of her status as a "famous" person in the literary world. The journal is not burdened by "inside" references or gossip about a narrow circle of literati. Sarton lives alone in a house near the sea in Maine, and she writes about her neighbors and friends as people who matter to her, not as people who relate to her only as May Sarton the famous author. The journal is peppered with references to mundane activities like shoveling a path through the snow to the bird feeder, taking her animals for walks, or struggling to keep red squirrels from getting inside her kitchen cabinets.

Readers of her journal will discover references to old age in the context of a life being lived day by day. Sarton does not dwell on old age as a primary topic. Many of her friends are people in their eighties and nineties. They represent old age to her. The deaths of two of these people close to her are reminders of her mortality, but when she evaluates her own age, she concludes, "It is plain that I am not ready for old age!"

Sarton, who is the author of numerous novels and books of poetry, has written several other journals, including *Plant Dreaming Deep, Journal of a Solitude,* and *After the Stroke.* See entries 124, 430, and 431 for annotations of her novel *As We Are Now* and her poems.

515 *Author:* Scott-Maxwell, Florida
Title: **The Measure of My Days**. New York: Knopf, 1968
Genre: nonfiction
Commentary: Scott-Maxwell, a playwright and Jungian analyst, wrote what she called this "note book" during her eighty-second year to find an outlet for her thinking about serious intellectual questions. Her journal is a record of her "measuring" her days,

grappling with several challenging issues and ideas that on the surface appear to have little to do with the experience of old age. For instance, she writes at length about the tensions between individuality and conformity, sameness and differentiation, and the individual versus the mass.

She writes, "We who are old know that age is more than a disability. It is an intense and varied experience, almost beyond our capacity at times, but something to be carried high." Other issues she raises in the journal: immortality ("You need only claim the events of your life to make yourself yours"), the relationship between good and evil, the meaning of love, the status of women, and the task of old age ("to endure must be our creative role. . . greatness is required of us").

She maintains that the primary task of old age is to add to and to clarify one's self, whatever the cost. She sums up her philosophy of life this way: "I want to tell people approaching and perhaps fearing age that it is a time of discovery. If they say—'Of what?' I can only answer, 'We must each find out for ourselves, otherwise it won't be discovery.'"

516 *Author:* Sheehan, Susan
Title: **Kate Quinton's Days.** New York: Houghton, 1984
Genre: nonfiction
Commentary: The limited resources, inflexible regulations, endless red tape, and the brutal inconsistency of the nation's health care system are exposed in this account of Kate Quinton, an 80-year-old widow, who lives with her daughter Claire in an apartment in a poor neighborhood in Brooklyn. Kate struggles to maintain her health and self–respect in the face of a recent hospitalization, recurring disabilities, tensions between family members, and a bureaucratic health-care system that prolongs her suffering and adds to her miseries rather than alleviating them.

Kate's story is told in the manner of an extended case study. Kate and Claire Quinton are pseudonyms for women the author interviewed for more than a year. In the first half of the book, Sheehan records numerous details of Kate's day-to-day existence after her hospitalization. Kate applies for Medicaid coverage, a process that takes more than six months. While Kate is waiting for her Medicaid application to be processed, she is placed in an experimental home health-care program funded by the city government.

But her placement in this program is undermined by the inconsistent and inefficient home health-care aides who are assigned to her case and by the unwarranted antagonism of a Medicaid case manager who tries to limit Kate's access to home health care and to delay the processing of her Medicaid application. For the first five months Kate and Claire endure repeated problems with fifteen different aides, who fail to complete all required physical tasks and often exhibit inappropriate social behaviors.

In the second half of the book, Sheehan includes detailed family histories that provide some perspective on Kate and Claire's lives. Readers learn that Kate is an Irish immigrant who worked most of her life as a domestic. Her husband died when she was 47, and her daughter Claire has lived with her for the last 20 years. Claire faces problems with a recurring disability and frequent bouts of depression. But Kate and Claire stay together through these difficult times.

The book ends one year after it began. Kate's life seems to improve when a new home health-care aide begins to work with her. But her physical and emotional ordeal still has not been resolved.

517 *Author:* Vining, Elizabeth Gray
  Title: **Being Seventy: The Measure of a Year.** New York: Viking, 1978
  Genre: nonfiction
  Commentary: This journal of the author's seventy-first year, from October 1972 to October 1973, contains many eloquent reflections on aging and death—all the more powerful for the author's being a sensitive and disciplined writer. For example:

> An old lady who has a genuine joy in living is an old lady who draws people to her. She is sufficient to herself. She has something to give—a gift the more precious and the more endearing because it is quite unconscious.

As Elizabeth Gray Vining contemplates moving into a retirement home (and finally commits herself to it), she works through many of the hesitations familiar to all who wonder about their final living arrangements.

During this year, Vining completes a biography of the Quaker poet Whittier, spends time in her Philadelphia home, travels to a literary conference in Japan, spends weeks at a writer's lodge on a Georgia island, and summers in New Hampshire. Widowed forty years ago in a happy marriage, she often thinks of those days. She is a distinguished older woman, an established author, recipient of honorary degrees, a college trustee. Her friendships are global. She also lives a vigorous and varied inner life marked by curiosity, wry humor, religious thoughtfulness, and kindliness. Her poetic observations of nature, seen in different seasons and climates, express an admirable contentment in simply *being*.

An important implication of the whole journal is that "being seventy" is no longer as near-the-end as it was. Much of this journal could have been written by a woman of fifty.

Major Life Responses

A natural and central question in reading about aged characters is, "How do these people handle life?" One comes to appreciate the scope of life attitudes that make old age frightening, piteous, exciting, inspiring—insights especially accessible through literature.

Eight large categories of life response are described below: Hate and Love; Fear and Courage; Disengagement and Engagement; Despair and Faith. For each, examples are given with cross-indexing to allow pursuit of a given theme.

(Numbers refer not to pages but to the numbered entries in the body of this text. The 100 series is assigned to novels, the 200s to short stories, the 300s to plays, the 400s to poems, the 500s to nonfiction.)

Hate

Old age can intensify lifelong conflicts. It can create new conflicts for people weakened in mind, body, and resources. Hatred toward the children is evidenced in the rage of Old Ben Brantly in Taylor's "Porte-Cochere" (259), in Tom Garrison's loveless domination of his son in Anderson's *I Never Sang for My Father* (301). (Also 121, 266, 267, 311, 507.) Marital hostility appears in the mother's deep resentment of her husband in Olsen's "Tell Me a Riddle" (247) and classically in the mutual antagonism of Tolstoy's "The Death of Ivan Ilyich" (262). (Also 102, 131, 250, 423.) Retirement home residents can dislike one another, as in Welty's "A Visit of Charity" (269), or their keepers, as in Updike's *Poorhouse Fair* (129). (Also 303.) The old may rage at age itself as in Harwood's *The Dresser* (306). (Also 113, 205.)

Grudges (128), spites (303), and deadlocks (233) display various angers. The pressures of aging can drive people deeper into their own selfishness, as with the repulsive immortal Struldbruggs of Swift's *Gulliver's Travels* (258; also 267) or the trivial self-gratifiers of Spark's *Memento Mori* (125). (Also 128, 224.) Hatred turned in upon itself becomes self-loathing, nowhere more horridly shown than in Beckett's *Krapp's Last Tape* (302). (Also 213, 237, 412, 414.)

Love

Love, affection, devotion—these life responses can enrich the late years, even strengthen them. In Mason's *Spence + Lila* (118) is seen the quiet steady fondness of a long-married husband and wife. Contentious but just as deep is the loving loyalty of Norman and Ethel Thayer in Thompson's *On Golden Pond* (312). (Also 126, 229, 257, 304, 307, 436, 443.) The caring of one spouse for the disabled other can be seen in Celia's support of her unemployed actor-husband in Woiwode's *Poppa John* (133). (Also 113, 310, 436.) Sexuality, including lust, does not necessarily fade, as Dr. Morris discovers in Malamud's "In Retirement" (234). (Also 106, 218, 224, 238, 414, 422, 446.) The one title dealing with homosexual attraction is Mann's "Death in Venice" (235). Age may bring new love—happily, as with Nathan's *The Color of Evening* (120), or tragically, as with Singer's "Old Love" (255). (Also 106, 110, 119, 205, 213, 226, 232, 248, 253.)

Affection within the family passes from generation to generation in Wilder's *The Long Christmas Dinner* (314). Grandparental devotion sustains the family in Cather's "Old Mrs. Harris" (212). (Also 240, 251, 270.) Sacrifice for loved ones is also seen in Gaines' *The Autobiography of Miss Jane Pittman* (112). (Also 211, 304.) Willy Loman's idolizing of his son Biff is a central strand of Miller's *Death of a Salesman* (310.) Freeman's "A Mistaken Charity" (222) shows the caring between two sisters. Hall's "Ideal Bakery" (223) shows the restorative power of an older man's memories of his father.

Reconciliation between the generations is the major possibility held forth in Fischer's *Growing Old in America* (507). (Also 245, 250, 266, 307, 308, 311, 312.) Enemies may reconcile, as in Minot's "Small Point Bridge" (239). Husbands may ask forgiveness, as in Williams' "Asphodel, That Greeny Flower" (443).

Friendship in old age proves a great resource in Munro's "Mrs. Cross and Mrs. Kidd" (241). (Also 106, 107, 123, 124, 227, 231, 249, 252, 305, 306, 313, 428, 517.) Intergenerational friendship provides mutual nurturing in old Mr. Sweet's playing with the children in Walker's "The Hell with Dying" (268). (Also 104, 105, 110, 111, 127, 132, 216, 225, 230, 244, 250, 261, 427.)

Fear

The shrinking resources of old age easily open one to anxiety, which comes close to panic for the frail widow trapped in her own bathtub in Frame's "The Bath" (221) or for the widower tricked into visiting a retirement home in Dokey's "The Autumn of Henry Simpson" (215). (Also 116, 126, 130, 264, 310, 312.) Fear can push one into dependence upon others, as in Frost's "The Death of the Hired Man" (410). (Also 208.) Symptoms of basic timidity would be aimlessness, postponement, or stagnation, as with the four aging office workers of Pym's *Quartet in Autumn* (122). (Also 117, 213, 219.)

Fear can drive one into eccentric exclusiveness, as with the retired colonel who shuns all forms of communication in Bates' "Where the Cloud Breaks" (204). It can hold one back from adventure (220), from new love (203, 217, 255), from new life in general (128, 260).

Courage

The nerve to hold fast no matter what comes is quietly illustrated by the gentlewoman who maintains her graciousness amid the confused boredoms of a retirement hotel in Elizabeth Taylor's *Mrs. Palfrey at the Claremont* (127). (Also 221, 263.) Self-reliance seems especially admirable in those of fading powers, as in the indomitable fisherman of Hemingway's *The Old Man and the Sea* (114). (Also 108, 222, 230, 253, 265, 270.) For endurance in old age, one might consult the solitary old man in Van Doren's "We Were Not Old" (437; also 105, 112, 516), or for endurance of terminal illness, one might consult others (118, 257, 502, 511).

Positive defiance is shown by the former teacher who rebels against elderly abuse in Sarton's *As We Are Now* (124) and by the widower who rebels against an over-protective daughter in Rosner's "Prize Tomatoes" (249). (Also 101, 123, 129, 214, 222, 252, 271, 272, 434.) Readiness for the remaining life is advocated in Cowley's *The View from 80* (506). (Also 413, 505.) An outright gusto for life is celebrated by the fast-talking champion of the downtrodden in Gardner's *I'm Not Rappaport* (305) and, of course, by the famous sailor-king of Tennyson's "Ulysses" (433). (Also 248, 260, 307, 309, 419, 427, 442, 445.)

Disengagement

Aging persons may let go of life gracefully, as Emerson counsels in "Terminus" (409). (Also 308, 413.) Or they may lament that life has let *them* go, lonely and abandoned. So the grandfather feels, in Steinbeck's "The Leader of the People" (256), when no one seems to value the pioneering achievement that has centered his life. (Also 262.) A grinding boredom marks the aimless retirement of Munsey Wills in Josephine Lawrence's *The Web of Time* (117). (Also 127, 129, 404.) An escape from the present through nostalgia for a happier past is taken by the bed-ridden mother of Brooks' "Jessie Mitchell's Mother" (403) and by the old colonel's flight into Confederate history in Shacochis' "Where Pelham Fell" (254). (Also 223, 246.)

A stubborn refusal to change has marked the later life of Hagar Shipley in Laurence's *The Stone Angel* (115). (Also 204, 205, 301.) The anxious farmer of Annabel Thomas' "Ashur and Evir" (260), who sinks his hopes and funds into a permanent care plan, illustrates withdrawal. (Also 203, 206, 220, 243, 445.) Dementia, Alzheimer's disease, general break-up—these constitute involuntary but nonetheless final departures from life's enterprises (130, 131, 202, 204, 207, 229, 236, 242, 246, 257, 258, 261, 401, 420, 425, 439, 508, 509). The ultimate disengagement, death, is abortively sought in the suicide plans of Knight's "The Resurrection Man" (228); it overtakes the author's mother in Beauvoir's *A Very Easy Death* (502). (Also 130, 131, 206, 210, 227, 246, 247, 251, 255, 262, 268, 405, 410, 424, 509, 511.)

Engagement

An active openness to life can make old age especially attractive, as it does in Harriet, the benevolent spirit of her nursing home in Bly's "Gunnar's Sword" (209). (Also 201.) Openness is prescribed in detail by Butler (504), Comfort (505), and Cowley (506), and is often illustrated by others (225, 408, 427, 433, 442, 513, 514, 517). Sometimes it shows, unhappily, as the unfulfilled yearning for a larger life, as in the starving crone of Berriault's "The Diary of K. W." (206). (Also 429.)

Adaptation as one way of keeping life open is imaginatively worked out by Olmstead in *Threshold: The First Days of Retirement* (512). (Also 118, 120, 122, 402, 505, 506.) One may seek challenges (433, 437). One may rebel against whatever narrows life, such as the speaker who determines to flout dull convention in Joseph's "Warning" (419). (Also 124, 129, 222, 247, 271, 411.) One may champion people or causes, like the old professor who undertakes to liberate an abused boy in Oates' "A Theory of Knowledge" (244). (Also 111, 216, 252, 263, 270, 305, 501, 504.)

Creativity in old age appears in all the women celebrated in Painter's *Gifts of Age* (513), in Koch's *I Never Told Anybody: Teaching Poetry Writing in a Nursing Home* (510). (Also 109, 119, 214, 268, 443, 445, 514, 517.) Age instead of narrowing may bring renewal, as in the rejuvenation of the drab residents in McEnroe's *The Silver Whistle* (309) or in Sylvia's "remaking" herself in Wilson's *Late Call* (132). (Also 103, 104, 120, 126, 248, 249, 255, 304, 431, 435, 514, 515.)

An ultimate engagement is to transmit one's values to the next generation, as the Irish teacher does in a time of terror in Trevor's "Attracta" (263). (Also 101, 240, 256, 314, 511.)

Despair

The light side of despair may be said to be vanity, a blind persistence in self-glorification, as with the ex-vaudevillian and parasitic father in Edwin O'Connor's "I Was Dancing" (121). (Also 125, 128, 246, 258, 306.)

A darker side is the unremitting pain of unresolved trauma, like that of Joe Allston in Stegner's *The Spectator Bird* (126), haunted by a son's death and an old romantic encounter. (Also 223, 426.) Remorse for his own failure darkens the last years of a one-time pornographic actor in Matthews' "The Eternal Mortgage" (237). (Also 133, 233, 432.)

Desolation and depression can descend after the loss of a loved one, as with the retired professor who loses a close friend in Johnson's "Old Harry" (227). (Also 115, 215, 231, 238, 255.) Despair can attend the loss of vocation or mission (116, 256). A general bleakness of life can produce a nonspecific wretchedness, as in the spiritually starved speaker in Roethke's "Old Lady's Winter Words" (429). (Also 107, 206, 302, 309, 516.) The hopelessness of many nursing home patients is conveyed in Wagoner's "Part Song" (438). (Also 130, 242, 401, 420, 439.) Finally, there is suicide (227, 228, 255, 310).

Faith

Spiritual conversion occurs most dramatically at the deathbed in Tolstoy's "The Death of Ivan Ilyich" (262) and again at the opening of John's hard old heart in Higgins' "The Courtship of Widow Sobcek" (226). (Also 245.) The search for life's meaning is central to Warren's "Ballad of Your Puzzlement" (440), pointing out the stumbling blocks to life review, and it is a major theme in many of these works, as with the questing millionaire invalid of Detre's *A Happy Ending* (110). (Also 114, 125, 132, 206, 213, 215, 310, 311, 418, 422.) An overlapping theme is the actual discovery of self. Thus Lady Slane in Sackville–West's *All Passion Spent* (123) finds in herself the real woman submerged in a lifetime of playing the statesman's wife. Florida Scott–Maxwell, keeping a journal of intellectual inquiry in *The Measure of My Days* (515), is another example. (Also 120, 209, 239, 244, 249, 430, 431, 440, 445.)

Faith already possessed is affirmed in Whitman's "Song at Sunset" (442) and Wheelock's "Song on Reaching Seventy" (441)—fine hymns to the goodness of life even in the final years. Active faith is demonstrated by Mattie, who in Christian spirit undertakes the care of a juvenile delinquent in Edgerton's *Walking Across Egypt* (111). (Also 211, 228, 263, 517.) The healing of others is exemplified by the grandfather who seeks to guide a disturbed boy in Mungoshi's "Who Will Stop the Dark?" (240). (Also 126, 133, 201.)

Faith may show itself in resolute fidelity to an ideal or a duty, as with Okonkwo, the tribal leader of Achebe's *Things Fall Apart* (101), who stands up tragically against the infiltration of white culture. (Also 127, 221, 263, 407.) Faith may live quietly as the simple trust in life expressed by D. H. Lawrence in "Shadows" (421). Also 409, 428, 430, 431.) It may simply express itself in a deep contentment, as with the affectionate old couple in Van Doren's "First Snow" (436). (Also 118, 212, 314, 415, 416.)

Anthologies

Middle Age, Old Age: Short Stories, Poems, Plays, and Essays on Aging. Ed. by Ruth Granetz Lyell. New York: HBJ, 1980.

An early anthology in this field but one of the most wide-ranging, Lyell's collection includes some 75 literary pieces: a score of short stories (with some folk tales), two-score poems, one play, and a half-dozen essays. Ruth Lyell, who has taught the psychology of aging, has also studied gerontology and draws on it in the documented essays that introduce each of the seven sections. She is particularly concerned to get beyond the narrow view that the aging process of our time and culture holds true for all times and societies. Therefore, she has drawn literary works from such cultures and periods as Biblical, Classical Greece and Rome, ancient and modern China and Japan, Renaissance, Arabic, Russia, India, modern France, Britain, and, of course, the United States. Middle age is also represented by a few pieces but not in an isolated way; it is seen as presenting some of the same challenges and difficulties that confront the later years. The length of selection ranges from extended—as for the whole two acts of Robert Anderson's *I Never Sang for My Father*—to brief poems and some excerpts. The seven sections bear these titles: Generational Relationships; Disappointment, The Life Review, and Unresolved Conflicts; Old Age as Wisdom and Peace; Loss; Dying and Death; Alone and with Peers; The Life Cycle.

The decades after the 1950s are thinly represented. In other respects, *Middle Age, Old Age* may be said to set a high standard for such collections. A new edition should be looked for.

Night Lights: Stories of Aging. Ed. by Constance Rooke. Toronto: Oxford Univ. Pr., 1986.

This collection of eleven stories and one reminiscence has unfortunately not been available in the United States. Its authors are generally well established. The majority of the selections date from pre-1970. They cover an unusual spread of locales: United States, Canada, Britain, Europe, Sri Lanka. All the protagonists are single. Old women are featured in nine selections, old men in three. A preface treats themes and symbolic associations.

Women and Aging: An Anthology by Women. Ed. by Jo Alexander and others. Corvallis, Ore: Calyx, 1986.

This avowedly feminist collection opposes ageism, especially as intensified for old women by sexism. It will enlighten those who have supposed ageism to mean the same thing for both sexes. It is comprehensive in genre: essays, photographs, stories, journals, poems, profiles, reviews, art works. Some one hundred pieces are here—a feature presumably expressing variety and the gathered force of many voices. For the most part, the writers, all American, do not have major literary reputations, although many have been published. They include many who have credentials as teachers, media workers, artists. An extensive bibliography lists literary works about women and aging, as well as periodicals, organizations, and art.

When I Am an Old Woman I Shall Wear Purple: An Anthology of Short Stories and Poetry. Ed. by Sandra Martz. Manhattan Beach, Calif.: Papier-Maché Pr., 1987.

Like *Women and Aging*, this collection concentrates on the female experience of aging. But it lacks the militant tone of that volume; it includes eight contributions by men. Several pieces, including the title poem, are delightfully lighthearted. Some fifty poems are here, a dozen pieces of fiction and a dozen photographs. As with *Women and Aging*, the contributors are Americans not widely known to the general public, although many have been published. Most have credentials as writers, teachers, media workers, artists. No preface or bibliography is provided.

Love Is Ageless: Stories about Alzheimer's Disease. Ed. by Jessica Bryan. Oakland, Calif: Serala Pr., 1987.

This specialized collection includes ten stories and fifteen poems that address Alzheimer's disease from varied viewpoints: health-care professionals, children of Alzheimer victims, friends, even the victims themselves. A dominant theme is that an encounter with an Alzheimer's victim is a devastating experience that changes a person's life forever. Alzheimer's disease, like old age or death, is a metaphor for the unknowable, what Sartre called the "other," the absolute mystery of our existence. Thus these stories, specialized as they are, invite an enlarged sensitivity to all the fragility of human life.

Full Measure: Modern Short Stories on Aging. Ed. by Dorothy Sennett, foreword by Carol Bly. St. Paul: Graywolf Pr., 1988.

These twenty-three stories, published between 1945 and 1985, concentrate on recent and contemporary American and British writers. Many have preeminent literary reputations, for example: Saul Bellow, John Cheever, Bernard Malamud, and Joyce Carol Oates. Dorothy Sennett writes in the preface that she wants the older people of these stories "to be of our time . . . and yet to reveal themselves . . . in all their extraordinary differences." Some stories deal with dying. Many deal with the "renewal" by which older people survive. We variously survive, Sennett suggests, through attachment to living things, attachment to places, attachment to the things we loved in the past, in the connectedness of generations, in those we love profoundly. The volume itself eludes any special ordering; each of its five sections shows a range of theme and mood.

Index
of Authors

Numbers refer not to pages but to the numbered entries in the body of the text. The 100 series is assigned to novels, the 200s to short stories, the 300s to plays, the 400s to poems, and the 500s to nonfiction.

Index
of Topics

Numbers refer not to pages but to the numbered entries in the body of the text. The 100 series is assigned to novels, the 200s to short stories, the 300s to plays, the 400s to poems, and the 500s to nonfiction.

For an index to specific life attitudes, also see Appendix 1.

Robert E. Yahnke is a professor of writing, literature, and film at the University of Minnesota. He is the author of *The Great Circle of Life: A Resource Guide to Films on Aging* for the National Health Publishing, and co-author of two bibliographies on literature and audiovisuals for the Association for Gerontology in Higher Education. Yahnke has also presented numerous papers and workshops at national conferences on the use of film and literature in gerontology. He is a graduate of the University of Wisconsin–Madison, with a doctorate in American literature.

Richard M. Eastman is professor emeritus of English at North Central College, Naperville, Illinois. He is the author of *Style: Writing and Reading as the Discovery of Outlook,* third edition (Oxford University Press). His article "Literary Windows on Aging" appeared in the *Loyola Psychiatric Forum* in 1988, and he is a freelance writer for several metropolitan newspapers. Eastman received his doctorate from the University of Chicago.